# *Baby Names*
## *An Essential Guide to Choosing the Perfect Name Including Thousands of Baby Names with Meaning and Origin*

advertising and all other aspects of doing business in the US, Canada, UK or any other jurisdiction is the sole responsibility of the purchaser or reader.

Neither the author nor the publisher assumes any responsibility or liability whatsoever on the behalf of the purchaser or reader of these materials. Any perceived slight of any individual or organization is purely unintentional.

# Contents

# Acknowledgements

After many, many long nights of going through databases, books, and other resources to compile our own database, we have a few people that we would like to give a special thanks to. Many people have helped us with the creation of this book but we especially want to thank Ronald Miller, Rosie Brown, and Marc Anderson. These people have contributed with their insights, wisdom, and recommended resources.

We also want to thank our kids Scarlett, Luke, and Emanuel who have been supporting from the start. Their grandparents; our wonderful parents are also very much appreciated. They've been in our corner from day one. And of course, thanks to all the business associates who have been better than best! It took us years to create this book, but without your help, we don't think that it would have been possible at all. Thank you all!

# Introduction

"What will the name be for my baby?" That is the question that inevitably arises for all parents. You start researching and thinking about possible names, but you can't quite decide which name you prefer. Perhaps your family and friends will offer you their opinion – whether it's wanted or unwanted. Maybe you feel stressed; time is running out as you go through week after week without any new insights.

If this sounds familiar, worry no more! This book is your essential guide to choosing the perfect name. Here, you can choose how you want to look for baby names. Do you prefer to look for only girl or boy names - or, do you prefer to look for both simultaneously so you can see counterparts of the name? Perhaps you prefer to search for names with a particular meaning? No matter your preference, we are confident that you will find what you need within this book. Sorted in alphabetical order, you got thousands of names with meaning and origin that you can go through. Some are popular; some are not. Some you will adore; some you will not. But the chances are that you will find this book useful and fun as you move closer to your goal of finding the perfect name!

So what are you waiting for? Turn over to the next page and start your journey now!

# Chapter 1 – How to Successfully Choose a name for your baby

This chapter will contain some guidelines and tips that can be great to follow when choosing the perfect name. Now, as parents ourselves, we know that you're most likely not looking for unwanted advice. Therefore, this book is not opinion based (except for the last chapter that contains reader's favorites). Instead, here are some factual and reasonable tips that can make you go "Ah, I never thought of that!"

1. **Say the name out loud.** Make sure that the name passes the verbal test. Are their any potential mispronunciations or unwanted attention that can be connected to this particular name?

2. **Look over initials.** Again, ask the questions mentioned in number 1. Also, think about potential emailhandles that can be generated from the initials. For example, the name Ajani Erkson can automatically become ajerk@yale.com.

3. **Think about the future.** Bunny or Binky might be cute names for a baby but what about a fifty year old man working in construction?

4. **Simple can be better.** An overcomplicated name can lead to frustration for the child. It can be wise to avoid giving your child the "excuse me, my name is actually..." phenomenon.

Alright, enough with tips. Let's get into the fun part, shall we? Turn to the next page to start your search for the perfect name.

# Chapter 3 – Popular Girl Names in 2017

♀ **Aaliyah**, Hebrew, Heavens, Exalted, Highborn
♀ **Abigail**, Hebrew, My father is joyful
♀ **Adalynn**, English, Noble guardian
♀ **Adeline**, English, Noble, Nobility
♀ **Alexa**, Greek, Defending men
♀ **Alexis**, Greek, Defender
♀ **Alice,** German, Noble
♀ **Allison**, German, Noble
♀ **Alyssa,** German, Noble
♀ **Amelia**, Hebrew, Work
♀ **Anna**, Hebrew, Grace
♀ **Annabelle**, Italian, Loving
♀ **Aria,** Latin, Air, Lioness
♀ **Ariana**, Welsh, Most holy
♀ **Arianna**, Greek, Very holy one
♀ **Ashley**, English, Dweller near the ash tree meadow
♀ **Athena**, Greek, Greek Goddess of wisdom
♀ **Aubree**, French, Elf ruler
♀ **Audrey**, German, Noble strenght
♀ **Aurora,** Latin, Dawn

- ♀ **Autumn**, Latin, Autumn
- ♀ **Ava,** Hebrew, Life
- ♀ **Bella,** Latin, Beautiful
- ♀ **Brianna,** Celtic, Strong, honourable and virtuous
- ♀ **Brooklyn**, English, Place-name
- ♀ **Camila,** French, Young ceremonial attendant
- ♀ **Caroline**, German, Free man
- ♀ **Charlotte,** Norse, Free man
- ♀ **Chloe**, Greek, Young green shoot
- ♀ **Claire,** Latin, Clear, bright
- ♀ **Delilah,** Hebrew, To flirt
- ♀ **Eleanor,** Hebrew, Pity (Greek meaning). God is my light (Arabic meaning
- ♀ **Elena,** Greek, Shining light, bright
- ♀ **Eliana,** Hebrew, My God has answered
- ♀ **Elizabeth**, Hebrew, Pledged to God
- ♀ **Ella,** French, Fairy maiden, All, Completly
- ♀ **Ellie,** Hebrew, Shining one, Bright
- ♀ **Emilia**, Latin, Rival; emulating (lating meaning). Industrious (Germanic meaning). Friendly; soft (Greek meaning).
- ♀ **Emily**, Latin, Rival
- ♀ **Emma**, Latin, Universal
- ♀ **Eva,** Hebrew, Life
- ♀ **Evelyn,** Celtic, Wished for child
- ♀ **Faith**, English, Belief, To trust

♀ **Gabriella**, Italian, God is my strenght
♀ **Gianna**, Hebrew, The Lord is gracious
♀ **Grace**, Latin, Grace of God, Beauty of form
♀ **Hailey**, English, Hay's meadow
♀ **Hannah**, Hebrew, Grace
♀ **Harper,** English, Harp player
♀ **Hazel,** English, The hazelnut tree
♀ **Isabella,** Hebrew, Pledged to God
♀ **Isabelle,** Hebrew, Pledged to God
♀ **Jade,** Spanish, Stone of the side
♀ **Jasmine**, Persian, Persian flowername
♀ **Julia,** Latin, Youthful
♀ **Katherine**, Greek, Pure
♀ **Kaylee**, Celtic, Laurel, Crown
♀ **Kylie**, Celtic, A boomerang
♀ **Layla**, Arabic, Night
♀ **Leah,** Hebrew, Weary
♀ **Liliana**, English, To climb like a vine
♀ **Lillian**, Hebrew, Lily, A Flower
♀ **Lily**, English, English flower name
♀ **Lucy**, Latin, Light
♀ **Luna,** Latin, Moon
♀ **Lydia**, Greek, Women from Lydia
♀ **Madeline**, Hebrew, Women from Magdala or high tower
♀ **Madelyn,** Hebrew, High tower or women from Magdala

♀ **Madison,** English, Son of Maud
♀ **Maya**, Sanskrit, Water
♀ **Melanie**, Greek, Dark, Black
♀ **Mia**, Latin, Mine; bitter
♀ **Mila,** Slavic, Diminutive of several European names
♀ **Naomi,** Hebrew, Pleasantness
♀ **Natalia,** Latin, Birthday of the Lord
♀ **Natalie**, Latin, Birthday of the Lord
♀ **Nevaeh**, English, Modern invented name
♀ **Nora,** Latin, Light
♀ **Olivia**, Latin, Olive tree
♀ **Paisley**, Gaelic, Church, cemetery
♀ **Penelope**, Greek, Weaver
♀ **Piper**, English, Flute player or piper
♀ **Ruby**, Latin, Deep red precious stone
♀ **Sadie**, Hebrew, Princess
♀ **Samantha**, English, Told by God
♀ **Sarah**, Hebrew, Princess
♀ **Savannah**, English, Flat tropical grassland
♀ **Scarlett,** English, Red
♀ **Serenity**, Latin, Peaceful
♀ **Skylar,** Dutch, Guarded, learned one (American meaning). Eternal life and strength (English meaning)
♀ **Sofia**, Greek, Wisdom
♀ **Sophia**, Greek, Wisdom
♀ **Stella**, Latin, Star

♀ **Trinity**, English, Triad
♀ **Valentina**, Latin, Health, Strenght
♀ **Victoria**, Latin, Victory
♀ **Violet,** Latin, Purple
♀ **Willow,** English, Willow tree
♀ **Zoe**, Greek, Life
♀ **Zoey**, Greek, Life

# Chapter 4 – Popular Boy Names in 2017

- ♂ **Aaron,** Hebrew, High mountain; enlightened, exalted
- ♂ **Adam,** Hebrew, Son of the red earth
- ♂ **Adrian,** Latin, Man of Adria
- ♂ **Aiden,** Celtic, Fiery and little
- ♂ **Alexander**, Greek, Defending men
- ♂ **Andrew**, Greek, Manly and strong
- ♂ **Angel,** Greek, Word name
- ♂ **Anthony**, English, Priceless one
- ♂ **Asher,** Hebrew, Happy one, Fortunate, Blessed
- ♂ **Austin**, Latin, Magnificent, Great
- ♂ **Ayden**, Celtic, Little fire
- ♂ **Benjamin,** Hebrew, son of the right hand
- ♂ **Bentley**, English, Meadow with coarse grass

- ♂ **Brandon**, English, Broom-covered hill
- ♂ **Brayden**, Celtic, Broad hill
- ♂ **Bryson**, Welsh, Son of Brice
- ♂ **Caleb**, Hebrew, Devotion to God
- ♂ **Cameron,** Celtic, Bent nose
- ♂ **Carson**, Celtic, Son of the marsh dwellers
- ♂ **Carter,** English, Driver or cart maker
- ♂ **Charles,** German, Free man
- ♂ **Chase,** English, To hunt
- ♂ **Christian,** Latin, Follower of Christ
- ♂ **Christopher,** Greek, Bearer of Christ
- ♂ **Colton**, English, From the coal or dark town
- ♂ **Connor**, Celtic, Lover of hounds
- ♂ **Cooper,** English, Barrel maker
- ♂ **Daniel,** Hebrew, God is my judge
- ♂ **David,** Hebrew, Beloved
- ♂ **Dominic**, Latin, Belonging to the lord
- ♂ **Dylan**, Welsh, Son of the sea
- ♂ **Easton**, English, East facing place
- ♂ **Eli**, Hebrew, Ascended, high, uplifted
- ♂ **Elias**, Hebrew, My God is the lord
- ♂ **Elijah**, Hebrew, Yahweh is God

- ♂ **Ethan**, Hebrew, Firm, strong
- ♂ **Evan,** Hebrew, The lord is gracious
- ♂ **Ezra,** Hebrew, Helper
- ♂ **Gabriel,** Hebrew, God is my strenght
- ♂ **Gavin,** Welsh, White hawk
- ♂ **Grayson**, English, The son of the baliff
- ♂ **Greyson**, English, Son of the steward
- ♂ **Henry**, German, Estate ruler
- ♂ **Hudson,** English, Son of Hugh
- ♂ **Hunter**, English, One who hunts
- ♂ **Ian**, Hebrew, The Lord is gracious
- ♂ **Isaac,** Hebrew, Laughter
- ♂ **Isaiah**, Hebrew, Salvation of the Lord
- ♂ **Jace**, Greek, Moon-Var. of Jason
- ♂ **Jack**, English, God is gracious
- ♂ **Jackson**, English, Son of Jack
- ♂ **Jacob**, Hebrew, Supplanter
- ♂ **James**, Hebrew, Supplanter
- ♂ **Jason,** Greek, To heal
- ♂ **Jaxon,** Greek, Jack's son
- ♂ **Jaxson,** English, Jack's son
- ♂ **Jayden**, Hebrew, God has heard
- ♂ **Jeremiah**, Hebrew, Appointed by God
- ♂ **John**, Hebrew, God is gracious

♂ **Jonathan,** Hebrew, Gift of Jehovah

♂ **Jordan**, Hebrew, Flowing down

♂ **Jose**, Spanish, Jehovah increases

♂ **Joseph**, Hebrew, Jehovah increases

♂ **Joshua,** Hebrew, The Lord is my salvation

♂ **Josiah**, Hebrew, Heals, God supports

♂ **Julian**, Latin, Downy, Youthful

♂ **Kayden**, Celtic, Battle, Son of Cadan

♂ **Kevin**, Celtic, Handsome

♂ **Landon,** English, Long hill

♂ **Leo,** Latin, Lion

♂ **Leonardo,** German, Brave lion

♂ **Levi,** Hebrew, Attached, joined

♂ **Liam**, German, Resolute protection

♂ **Lincoln,** English, Town by the pool

♂ **Logan**, Celtic, Little hollow

♂ **Lucas**, Latin, Man from Luciana

♂ **Luke**, Greek, Man from Luciana

♂ **Mason**, French, Stoneworker

♂ **Mateo,** Hebrew, Gift of God

♂ **Matthew**, Hebrew, Gift of God

♂ **Michael**, Hebrew, Who is like God?

♂ **Nathan,** Hebrew, Given

- ♂ **Nicholas,** Greek, People of Victory
- ♂ **Noah,** Hebrew, Comfort, Rest
- ♂ **Nolan**, Celtic, Champion
- ♂ **Oliver**, German, Olive tree
- ♂ **Owen**, Welsh, Well-born; young warrior
- ♂ **Parker**, French, Park keeper
- ♂ **Robert,** German, Bright fame
- ♂ **Roman**, Latin, Citizen of Rome
- ♂ **Ryan,** Celtic, Little king
- ♂ **Samuel**, Hebrew, Told by God
- ♂ **Santiago**, Latin, Saint James
- ♂ **Sebastian,** German, From the ancient city of Sebasta
- ♂ **Thomas,** Aramaic, Twin
- ♂ **Tyler**, English, Maker of tiles
- ♂ **William,** German, Resolute protection
- ♂ **Wyatt,** English, Brave in war
- ♂ **Xavier,** Basque, Bright or new house
- ♂ **Zachary**, Hebrew, The Lord has remembered

# Chapter 5 – Girl Baby Names Sorted By Meaning

## *Meaning: Angel*

- ♀ **Angel**, Origin: Greek
- ♀ **Angela**, Origin: Greek, French, Mexican
- ♀ **Angelica**, Origin: Latin, Greek
- ♀ **Angelina**, Origin: Greek, Latin
- ♀ **Angeline,** Origin: French, Latin, Russian
- ♀ **Angelique**, Origin: French, Greek
- ♀ **Angie**, Origin: Greek, Latin
- ♀ **D'Angela**, Origin: American
- ♀ **Dangelo**, Origin: Italian, Greek
- ♀ **Gina**, Origin: Greek, Italian
- ♀ **Heaven**, Origin: American, English
- ♀ **Serafina**, Origin: Spanish, Hebrew

♀ **Seraphim**, Origin: Hebrew
♀ **Tang**i, Origin: American
♀ **Zeraphina,** Origin: Hebrew

## Meaning: Happy

- ♀ **Ada**, Origin: Teutonic, Hebrew, English
- ♀ **Adamaris**, Origin: American
- ♀ **Alaia**, Origin: Arabic, Basque
- ♀ **Bea,** Origin: American, English
- ♀ **Beatrice**, Origin: Latin
- ♀ **Beatrix**, Origin: English, Latin
- ♀ **Blythe**, Origin: English
- ♀ **Desdemona**, Origin: Greek
- ♀ **Felice**, Origin: Italian, Latin
- ♀ **Felicia,** Origin: Latin
- ♀ **Felicity**, Origin: Latin, English
- ♀ **Gaye**, Origin: English
- ♀ **Keiko**, Origin: Japanese
- ♀ **Merry**, Origin: English
- ♀ **Radhiya,** Origin: African, Swahili
- ♀ **Sharmila,** Origin: Hindi, Indian
- ♀ **Trixie,** Origin: English, Latin

# *Meaning: Peace*

- ♀ **Alana**, Origin: Celtic, Old German, Irish
- ♀ **Amandeep**, Origin: Sanskrit
- ♀ **Chesney**, Origin: French, English
- ♀ **Dove**, Origin: English
- ♀ **Fia**, Origin: Italian, Scottish
- ♀ **Frederica**, Origin: Teutonic, German
- ♀ **Frida,** Origin: Teutonic, German
- ♀ **Frieda,** Origin: Teutonic, German
- ♀ **Iraina,** Origin: Russian
- ♀ **Irene,** Origin: Greek
- ♀ **Jerusalem,** Origin: Hebrew
- ♀ **Lana,** Origin: Celtic, Old German, English
- ♀ **Luba**, Origin: Polish
- ♀ **Malia,** Origin: Hebrew, Hawaiian
- ♀ **Malu**, Origin: Hawaiian
- ♀ **Naima,** Origin: Arabic
- ♀ **Noa**, Origin: Hebrew
- ♀ **Noah,** Origin: Hebrew
- ♀ **Noé,** Origin: Hebrew
- ♀ **Pace,** Origin: English
- ♀ **Pacifica**, Origin: Spanish
- ♀ **Pax,** Origin: Latin

♀ **Paz,** Origin: Hebrew, Spanish
♀ **Peace**, Origin: English
♀ **Salomé,** Origin: Hebrew
♀ **Selima,** Origin: Hebrew
♀ **Serena,** Origin: Latin
♀ **Serenity,** Origin: English, Latin
♀ **Shalom**, Origin: Hebrew
♀ **Shanti,** Origin: Sanskrit
♀ **Shiloh,** Origin: Hebrew
♀ **Winifred,** Origin: Celtic, German
♀ **Yen,** Origin: Vietnamese
♀ **Zell,** Origin: Hebrew

# *Meaning: Happy*

- ♀ **Ada,** Origin: Teutonic, Hebrew, English
- ♀ **Adamaris**, Origin: American
- ♀ **Alaia,** Origin: Arabic, Basque
- ♀ **Bea**, Origin: American, English
- ♀ **Beatrice,** Origin: Latin
- ♀ **Beatrix,** Origin: English, Latin
- ♀ **Blythe,** Origin: English
- ♀ **Desdemona**, Origin: Greek
- ♀ **Felice,** Origin: Italian, Latin
- ♀ **Felicia,** Origin: Latin
- ♀ **Felicity,** Origin: Latin, English
- ♀ **Gaye**, Origin: English
- ♀ **Keiko,** Origin: Japanese
- ♀ **Merry**, Origin: English
- ♀ **Radhiya**, Origin: African, Swahili
- ♀ **Sharmila,** Origin: Hindi, Indian
- ♀ **Trixie,** Origin: English, Latin

# Meaning: Love

♀ **Aimee,** Origin: French
♀ **Amanda**, Origin: Latin
♀ **Amara**, Origin: Greek
♀ **Amoretta,** Origin: Latin
♀ **Amy**, Origin: French, Portuguese, Latin
♀ **Aphrodite**, Origin: Greek
♀ **Brisa**, Origin: Spanish
♀ **Caris**, Origin: Welsh
♀ **Carissa**, Origin: French, Greek
♀ **Ceridwen**, Origin: Welsh
♀ **Cerie**, Origin: Welsh
♀ **Cher**, Origin: French
♀ **Cheri,** Origin: French
♀ **Cherish,** Origin: English
♀ **Davida,** Origin: Hebrew
♀ **Derica,** Origin: Teutonic, German
♀ **Didi**, Origin: Hebrew
♀ **Dodie**, Origin: Hebrew
♀ **Esmé,** Origin: French
♀ **Filippa**, Origin: Greek
♀ **Gael**, Origin: Celtic, English, Greek
♀ **Gertrude**, Origin: Teutonic, German
♀ **Habiba**, Origin: Arabic

♀ **Halia,** Origin: Greek, Hawaiian
♀ **Heart**, Origin: English
♀ **Kalila,** Origin: Arabic
♀ **Karissa,** Origin: Greek
♀ **Kyla**, Origin: Celtic, Scottish, Hebrew
♀ **Laramie,** Origin: French
♀ **Leba**, Origin: Yiddish
♀ **Lida,** Origin: Russian, Slavic
♀ **Ludmilla,** Origin: Russian, Slavic
♀ **Maite,** Origin: Spanish
♀ **Myrna,** Origin: Arabic, Celtic, Irish
♀ **Nahid,** Origin: Persian
♀ **Nayeli**, Origin: American, Latin, Native American
♀ **Pandora,** Origin: Greek
♀ **Paris,** Origin: Greek, French
♀ **Phillipa,** Origin: Greek
♀ **Pleasant**, Origin: English
♀ **Sherry**, Origin: Hebrew, English, French
♀ **Suki,** Origin: Japanese
♀ **Taffy,** Origin: Welsh
♀ **Tanith,** Origin: African, Phoenician
♀ **Thandie,** Origin: African
♀ **Venus**, Origin: Greek, Latin
♀ **Xylophia,** Origin: Greek
♀ **Yaretzi**, Origin: Aztec, American

## *Meaning: Princess*

- ♀ **Amira**, Origin: Arabic, Hebrew
- ♀ **Damita**, Origin: Spanish
- ♀ **Elmira**, Origin: Arabic
- ♀ **Sadie,** Origin: Hebrew
- ♀ **Sally**, Origin: Hebrew, English
- ♀ **Sarah,** Origin: Hebrew
- ♀ **Sarahi**, Origin: Hebrew
- ♀ **Sarai,** Origin: Hebrew
- ♀ **Sari,** Origin: Arabic, Hebrew
- ♀ **Sariah,** Origin: Hebrew
- ♀ **Sarita**, Origin: Indian, Hebrew
- ♀ **Soraya**, Origin: Persian
- ♀ **Suri**, Origin: Persian, Hebrew
- ♀ **Tia**, Origin: Greek, Spanish
- ♀ **Tiana,** Origin: Greek, Latin
- ♀ **Zadie,** Origin: English
- ♀ **Zara,** Origin: Arabic, Hebrew
- ♀ **Zaria,** Origin: Russian, Latin, Hebrew

# *Meaning: Beautiful*

♀ **Alika**, Origin: Swahili
♀ **Aloha**, Origin: Hawaiian
♀ **Anahi**, Origin: Persian, Spanish
♀ **Annabella**, Origin: Latin, English
♀ **Anwen,** Origin: Welsh
♀ **Arabella**, Origin: English, Latin
♀ **Beila**, Origin: French, Spanish
♀ **Belinda**, Origin: Latin, Spanish
♀ **Bella**, Origin: Hebrew, Latin
♀ **Bellamy**, Origin: French
♀ **Belle**, Origin: French
♀ **Belva,** Origin: Latin
♀ **Calista,** Origin: Greek
♀ **Calla,** Origin: Greek
♀ **Callalily**, Origin: Greek
♀ **Calliope,** Origin: Greek
♀ **Christabel**, Origin: English, Latin
♀ **Clarabell,** Origin: Latin
♀ **Eavan,** Origin: Celtic, Gaelic
♀ **Ella,** Origin: English
♀ **Ella,** Origin: Spanish, English, Greek
♀ **Farrah,** Origin: English
♀ **Gamila**, Origin: Arabic
♀ **Hermosa**, Origin: Spanish
♀ **Hiraani**, Origin: Hawaiian
♀ **Ilona**, Origin: Greek, Hungarian

♀ **Jaffa**, Origin: Hebrew
♀ **Jamilla**, Origin: Arabic
♀ **Kalidas**, Origin: Greek
♀ **Kelis**, Origin: American
♀ **Kennis,** Origin: Gaelic
♀ **Kimi,** Origin: Japanese
♀ **Kunani,** Origin: Hawaiian
♀ **Lulabelle**, Origin: American
♀ **Maribel**, Origin: Spanish, Mexican, French
♀ **Mieko,** Origin: Japanese
♀ **Mika,** Origin: Japanese
♀ **Miki**, Origin: Japanese
♀ **Mirabella,** Origin: Latin
♀ **Navit,** Origin: Hebrew
♀ **Nefertiti**, Origin: Egyptian, Ancient Egyptian
♀ **Olathe,** Origin: Native American
♀ **Rosabelle**, Origin: French, Italian
♀ **Rupali,** Origin: Indian
♀ **Shayna,** Origin: Yiddish, Hebrew
♀ **Shifra**, Origin: Hebrew
♀ **Sohna**, Origin: Indian
♀ **Teagan**, Origin: Celtic, Irish, Welsh
♀ **Trixibelle**, Origin: American
♀ **Vashti,** Origin: Persian
♀ **Yaffa**, Origin: Hebrew
♀ **Yamilla,** Origin: Arabic
♀ **Zaina,** Origin: Arabic
♀ **Zaniah,** Origin: Arabic

# Chapter 6 – Boy Baby Names Sorted By Meaning

## *Meaning: King*

- ♂ **Ara**, Origin: Armenian, American, Arabic
- ♂ **Balthazar,** Origin: English, Greek
- ♂ **Basil,** Origin: Greek
- ♂ **Common,** Origin: English
- ♂ **Delroy**, Origin: French
- ♂ **Elroy,** Origin: French
- ♂ **Eze**, Origin: African
- ♂ **Kendrick**, Origin: English, Welsh
- ♂ **Kenwood**, Origin: English
- ♂ **Kingsley,** Origin: English
- ♂ **Kingston,** Origin: English
- ♂ **Kinsley**, Origin: English, Celtic, American
- ♂ **LeBron**, Origin: African
- ♂ **Leroy**, Origin: French, Portuguese

♂ **Melchior**, Origin: Arabic
♂ **Naresh,** Origin: Indian, Hindi
♂ **Obba**, Origin: Yoruban
♂ **Pippin,** Origin: French, German
♂ **Pomeroy**, Origin: French
♂ **Prince,** Origin: Latin
♂ **Ray**, Origin: French, Old German
♂ **Rex**, Origin: Latin
♂ **Rey**, Origin: French, Spanish
♂ **Reynaldo**, Origin: Teutonic, Spanish
♂ **Reynolds**, Origin: Celtic, English
♂ **Roy**, Origin: Celtic, Irish, French
♂ **Ryan**, Origin: Celtic, Irish
♂ **Ryne,** Origin: American, Irish
♂ **Wassili,** Origin: Greek
♂ **Waverly**, Origin: English

# Meaning: Handsome

- ♂ **Alan,** Origin: Celtic, Old German, Irish
- ♂ **Beau,** Origin: French
- ♂ **Beauregard**, Origin: French
- ♂ **Bello**, Origin: French
- ♂ **Cavan**, Origin: Celtic, Irish
- ♂ **Cullen**, Origin: Celtic, Irish
- ♂ **Hassan**, Origin: Arabic
- ♂ **Jamal,** Origin: Arabic
- ♂ **Jamar,** Origin: African, Arabic
- ♂ **Jamari**, Origin: French, Arabic
- ♂ **Jamel**, Origin: Arabic
- ♂ **Jamil**, Origin: Arabic
- ♂ **Jamir**, Origin: Arabic
- ♂ **Japheth**, Origin: Hebrew
- ♂ **Kavan**, Origin: Celtic, Irish
- ♂ **Kavanaugh**, Origin: Irish
- ♂ **Keane**, Origin: English, Celtic
- ♂ **Kenna,** Origin: Celtic, Scottish, Irish
- ♂ **Kenneth,** Origin: Celtic, Scottish, Irish
- ♂ **Kevin,** Origin: Celtic, Irish
- ♂ **Shaquille**, Origin: African, Arabic

♂ **Wasim,** Origin: Arabic
♂ **Yahir,** Origin: American, Arabic
♂ **Yamil,** Origin: Arabic
♂ **Yaphet**, Origin: Hebrew

# *Meaning: Man*

♂ **Abraham,** Origin: Hebrew
♂ **Adam**, Origin: Hebrew
♂ **Alexander,** Origin: Greek
♂ **Almanzo**, Origin: Old German
♂ **Anders,** Origin: Greek, Scandinavian
♂ **Andreas**, Origin: Teutonic, Greek
♂ **Andrew**, Origin: Greek
♂ **Ansel**, Origin: French, German
♂ **Apollo,** Origin: Greek
♂ **Archer,** Origin: English
♂ **Armand**, Origin: Teutonic, German
♂ **Armando,** Origin: Teutonic, German, Spanish
♂ **Bolton**, Origin: English
♂ **Bono,** Origin: Latin
♂ **Butch,** Origin: American
♂ **Bwana**, Origin: Swahili
♂ **Carl**, Origin: English, Teutonic, Old German, German
♂ **Cartman**, Origin: English
♂ **Charles**, Origin: Teutonic, Old German, German
♂ **Declan**, Origin: Celtic, Gaelic, Irish
♂ **Dermot,** Origin: Celtic, Irish

♂ **Desmond**, Origin: Celtic, Irish, Gaelic

♂ **Destry**, Origin: French, English

♂ **Duke**, Origin: English, French

♂ **Earl,** Origin: Celtic, English, Old English

♂ **Edgar,** Origin: English, Old English

♂ **Ellsworth**, Origin: Hebrew, English

♂ **Eugene**, Origin: Greek

♂ **Eugenie**, Origin: Greek

♂ **Fabrice**, Origin: Italian

♂ **Fabrizio**, Origin: Italian

♂ **Fisher**, Origin: English, Old English

♂ **Flynn**, Origin: Celtic, Irish

♂ **Forsythe**, Origin: Gaelic

♂ **Foster**, Origin: English

♂ **Francesco**, Origin: Latin, Italian

♂ **Freeman,** Origin: English

♂ **Garrett**, Origin: English, Old German, Irish

♂ **Gatlin**, Origin: English

♂ **Gavrie,** Origin: Russian

♂ **Gerard,** Origin: Teutonic, English

♂ **Gerardo**, Origin: Spanish, German

♂ **Germaine**, Origin: French

♂ **German**, Origin: Spanish, French, English

♂ **Gregor,** Origin: Greek, Dutch

♂ **Gregory**, Origin: Greek, Latin

♂ **Howard**, Origin: English, Old English

♂ **Ibrahim**, Origin: Arabic, Hebrew

♂ **Janus**, Origin: Latin

♂ **Jarvis**, Origin: English, Old English, German

♂ **Jermaine**, Origin: Latin

♂ **Jerry**, Origin: Greek, English, German

♂ **Jove,** Origin: Latin, Greek

♂ **Kale**, Origin: Hawaiian

♂ **Karl**, Origin: Teutonic, German

♂ **Lenno,** Origin: Native American

♂ **Mackean,** Origin: Scottish

♂ **Macleod**, Origin: English, Gaelic

♂ **Manfred,** Origin: Teutonic, English

♂ **Manley,** Origin: English

♂ **Manning,** Origin: English

♂ **Manny,** Origin: Spanish, English

♂ **Manzie,** Origin: American

♂ **Marques,** Origin: Spanish, Portuguese

♂ **Marquis,** Origin: French

♂ **Medgar**, Origin: German

♂ **Oscar,** Origin: English, Old English, Scandinavian

♂ **Paine**, Origin: Latin

♂ **Patrick,** Origin: Latin

♂ **Pompey**, Origin: Latin

♂ **Quenby,** Origin: Scandinavian

♂ **Quimby,** Origin: Scandinavian

♂ **Richard**, Origin: English, Old German

♂ **Rodman,** Origin: English, German

♂ **Roger**, Origin: English, Old German, German
♂ **Romany**, Origin: Romany
♂ **Rutger**, Origin: Dutch, Scandinavian
♂ **Ryder**, Origin: English, Old English
♂ **Saxon,** Origin: English
♂ **Steadman**, Origin: English
♂ **Thurgood,** Origin: English
♂ **Truman,** Origin: English
♂ **Wayman**, Origin: English
♂ **Wentworth**, Origin: English
♂ **Whit**, Origin: English
♂ **Whitman,** Origin: English
♂ **Yancey**, Origin: Native American

## *Meaning: Strong*

♂ **Anders**, Origin: Greek, Scandinavian

♂ **Andrea**, Origin: Greek

♂ **Andreas**, Origin: Teutonic, Greek

♂ **Andrew,** Origin: Greek

♂ **Armstrong**, Origin: English

♂ **Barrett**, Origin: English, German

♂ **Boaz,** Origin: Hebrew

♂ **Bogart,** Origin: Teutonic, French

♂ **Brian,** Origin: Celtic, Irish, Scottish

♂ **Charles,** Origin: Teutonic, Old German, German

♂ **Charlie,** Origin: Teutonic, Old German, German

♂ **Djimon**, Origin: West African

♂ **Durell**, Origin: English, French

♂ **Eberhard,** Origin: Teutonic, German

♂ **Ekon,** Origin: Nigerian
♂ **Ellard**, Origin: Teutonic, German
♂ **Emmett**, Origin: English, German
♂ **Etai**, Origin: Hebrew
♂ **Ethan**, Origin: Hebrew
♂ **Ezra**, Origin: Hebrew
♂ **Fergus**, Origin: Celtic, Irish
♂ **Gerrit**, Origin: Teutonic, Dutch
♂ **Humberto**, Origin: Teutonic, Portuguese
♂ **Kemen**, Origin: Spanish, Basque
♂ **Kwan**, Origin: Chinese, Korean
♂ **Neon**, Origin: Greek
♂ **Plato**, Origin: Greek
♂ **Quigley**, Origin: Celtic, Irish
♂ **Quinlan**, Origin: Celtic, Irish
♂ **Ragnar**, Origin: English, Scandinavian
♂ **Raynor**, Origin: English, Scandinavian
♂ **Remo**, Origin: English, Greek
♂ **Richmond**, Origin: Teutonic, German
♂ **Valentin**, Origin: Spanish, Latin
♂ **Valentino**, Origin: Italian
♂ **Valeria**, Origin: Italian, Latin
♂ **Valerie**, Origin: French, Latin
♂ **Valery**, Origin: Russian, Latin
♂ **Willard**, Origin: Teutonic, German

# Chapter 7 – Both Girl and Boy Names Sorted in Alphabetical order

Here is list of both boy and girl names combined with meaning and origin sorted in alphabetical order. A lot of our readers requested that one list should not be sorted by gender so that they could easily find the female or male counterpart of the name. Some of the counterparts are found right next to the name in bold, while others are below or above. You can also see the origin for most names as well as the innate meaning and spiritual association. We sincerely hope that you'll enjoy the list, best of lucks!

## *A*

- **Aaron**, Danish, Eagle, Perseverance
- **Abiel,** Abielle, Hebrew, Child of God, Heir of the Kingdom
- **Abram**, Hebrew, Father of Nations, Founder
- **Abriel**, Abrielle French Innocent Tenderhearted
- **Ace**, Latin Unity One With the Father

- **Acton**, Akton, Old English, Oak-Tree Settlement, Agreeable
- **Ada**, Adah, Adalee, Aida, Hebrew, Ornament, One Who Adorns
- **Adam,** Hebrew, Formed of Earth, In God's Image
- **Adaya**, Hebrew, God's Jewel, Valuable
- **Addison,**
- **Adeline**, Adalina, Adella,
- **Adelle**, Adelynn, Old German, Noble, Under God's Guidance
- **Adelyn**, Hebrew, Honor, Courageous
- **Adia,** African Gift, Gift of Glory
- **Adiel**, Addiel, Addielle, Hebrew, Ornament of God, Lovely
- **Adina**, Hebrew, Adorned, Clothed With Praise
- **Adisson**, Old English Son of Adam In God's Image
- **Adonijah**, Adonia,
- **Adora**, Adoree, Latin, Beloved, Gift of God
- **Adreyan**, Adriaan,
- **Adria,** Latin, Love of Life, Filled With Life
- **Adrian**, Adreian,
- **Adriann**, Adianne,
- **Adrianna**, Adriana Italian Dark Guarded of God

- **Adriel,** Hebrew, Member of Gods Flock, Nurtured of God
- **Adrien**, Adriene Greek Confident Faith in God
- **Adrien**, Adrion, Adryan,
- **Adrienne**, Adriane,
- **Adryon,** Greek, Rich, Prosperous
- **Agnes**,
- **Agnessa**, Greek, Pure, Innocent
- **Aiesha**, Aesha, Aisha,
- **Aileen**, Ailean, Ailene,
- **Ailina**, English, Light Bearer, Messenger of Truth
- **Aimie**, Aimmie, Aimy,
- **Aladdin**, Middle Eastern, Pinnacle of Faith, Righteous
- **Alan**, Al, Allan, Alen
- **Albert**, Al, Alberto, Elbert, Old English, Noble Brilliant
- **Aldis**, Anglo-Saxon, Wise Protector, Guided of God
- **Alea**, Aleah, Aleea,
- **Aleck**, Aleksandar,
- **Alecksander**, Alexandar,
- **Alejandro,** Alejandra,
- **Aleksi**, Alexes, Alexis,
- **Alex**, Alexia, Allex, Allix,
- **Alexa,** Aleksa, Aleksia,
- **Alexander**, Alax, Alec,
- **Alexandra**, Aleksandra,
- **Alexandria**, Lexandra, Greek, Defender of Mankind, Generous

- **Alexandros**, Alexius,
- **Alexis,** Aleksei, Aleksey,
- **Alexxander,**  Greek Defender of Mankind, Brave Protector
- **Alfonso**, Alfonzo,
- **Ali,** Swahili, Exalted, Greatest
- **Alianna**, Scottish, Bearer of Light, Ambassador of Truth
- **Alice**, Alis, Allis, Alysse, Greek, One of Integrity, Truthful
- **Alicia**, Alica, Alicea,
- **Alim**, Aleem Middle Eastern Scholar Wise
- **Aline,** Old German, Noble, Righteous
- **Alisa**, Alissa, Allissa,
- **Alisha**, Aleasha,
- **Allan**, Alan, Irish Harmonious At One With Creation
- **Allastair**, Allaster, Allastir,
- **Allegra**, Alegrea,
- **Allegrea,** Latin, Cheerful, Eager to Live
- **Allen**, Irish Harmonious At One With Creation
- **Allie**, Anglo-Saxon Brilliant Illuminated
- **Allison**, Alicen, Alicyn,
- **Allysa,** English, Noble, Bold
- **Allyson**, Old German, Truthful, Holy

- **Allyster**, Scottish, Defender, Courage
- **Almeira**, Middle Eastern, Princess, Fulfillment of Truth
- **Alonzo,**
- **Alpha**, Phoenician, Ox, Restful
- **Althea,** Greek, Healer, Wholesome
- **Alva**, (see also Elva), Latin, Brightness, Alive
- **Alvin**, Al, Alvan, Alven,
- **Alvis**, (see also Elvis) Scandinavian All-Knowing Conqueror
- **Alvyn**. German, Friend of All, Sincere
- **Alyssa**, (see Alisa)
- **Alyx,** Allyx Hungarian Defender of Mankind Benefactor
- **Amada**, Amadea,
- **Amadeo**, Latin, Lover of God, Obedient
- **Amadeus**,
- **Amanda**, Amandah,
- **Amber**, Ambur, (see also
- **Amelia**, Amaley, Amalia,
- **Amery**, Aimery, Ameri,
- **Amie**, Ammy, Latin, Beloved, Serene Spirit
- **Amira**, Hebrew, Speech, Unhidden
- **Amiran**, Ameiran
- **Amos,** Hebrew, Bearer of Burden, Compassionate
- **Amy**, Aimee, Aimey,

- **Andrea**, Andee, Andi,
- **Andrei**, Andres, Andy,
- **Andreia**, Andreya, Andria Greek Womanly Filled With Grace
- **Andrew**,
- **Angela**, Angee, Angel,
- **Angelea,**
- **Angeliana**, Angelina,
- **Angeline**,
- **Angelo**, Italian, Angel/Messenger, Bringer of Glad Tidings
- **Angi**, Greek, Angel/Messenger, Bringer of Glad Tidings
- **Angie**, Angelena,
- **Ani**, Hawaiian, Beautiful, Lovely in Spirit,
- **Ann**, Anne, Annette,
- **Anna,** Gracious, Full of Grace
- **Annabell**, Latin, Graceful, Beloved
- **Anni,**
- **Annika,** Czech, Favor, Grace of God
- **Anson**, Old German, Divine, Partaker in Glory
- **Anthoney**, Anthonie,
- **Anthony**, Anfernee,
- **Antoine**, Antony, (see
- **Anton**, Slavic One of Value, Eloquent
- **Antonette**, Antonia, Russian Favor of God, Peace
- **Antonia**, Antoinette,

- **Antonio**, Antonius, Italian, Priceless, Righteous
- **Ardelle**, Ardella, Latin, Eager, Spirit of Praise
- **Ardon**, Ardan, Arden,
- **Arial**, Ariale, Arielle,
- **Ariana**, Aeriana, Arianna,
- **Ariel**, Aerial, Aeriell,
- **Arienne**, Greek, Holy, Presented to God
- **Aristotle**, Ari, Arias, Arie,
- **Ariyel,**
- **Arlene**, Arlana, Arleen,
- **Armand,** Armando,
- **Arni**, Arnie, Old German, Strong as an Eagle, Brave
- **Arnold**, Arne, Arney,
- **Aron**, Arran, Arron, Hebrew, Light Bringer Radiating, God's Light
- **Arric**, Old German, Joyful, Spirit of Joy
- **Asa,** Hebrew, Healer, Healer of the Mind
- **Asha**, Middle Eastern, Vitality, Humble Strength
- **Ashby**, English, From the Ash-Tree Farm, Fear of God
- **Asheleigh**, Asheley,
- **Ashlea**,
- **Ashleigh**, Old English, Of the Ash-Tree Meadow, Harmony
- **Ashlen**, Ashlin, Ashling,

- **Ashley**, Ashelee,
- **Ashlyn**, Ashlyne,
- **Ashlynn**
- **Ashton**, English, From the Ash-Tree Farm, Supplicant
- **Asreel,** Asreyel
- **Asriel,**
- **Asriel**, Hebrew, God Helped, Delivered
- **Athena**, Athina Greek Wise Mind of God
- **Atleigh,** English, From the Meadow, Purchased
- **Atwell,** Attwell, English, From the Well, Refreshing
- **Aubrey,** Aubray,
- **Audie**, Old English, Property Guardian, Strong of Heart
- **Audrey**, Audra, Audray,
- **Audrianna**, Old English, Noble Strength, Overcomer of Many Difficulties
- **Augustine,** Latin, Venerable, Exalted
- **Augustus**, August,
- **Aurel**, Aurele, Aurelio, Czech, From Aurek, Reverent
- **Aurielle,** Latin, Golden, Sealed
- **Aurora**, Aurore, Latin, Dawn, Mouthpiece of God
- **Austin**, Austan, Austen,

- **Austyn**, Latin, Renowned, Guided of God
- **Ava**, Hebrew, From the Palace, Blessed
- **Avery**, Averey, Averie Middle Eastern Ruler Wise Counselor
- **Avis**, Avia, Aviana, Latin, Refuge, Place of Freedom
- **Axel,**
- **Azarel,**

## B

- **Baden**, Hebrew, Son of Judgment, Encourager
- **Bailey**, Bailee, Bailie,
- **Bain**, Baine
- **Baker**, see Baxter
- **Bali**, Baylee, Bayley,
- **Balin,** Baylin
- **Bambi**, Bambee, Bambie, Italian, Child, Innocent
- **Bane**, Gaelic, Fair, Cleansed
- **Bane**, Bayne
- **Bannie**, Hebrew, Built, Honorable
- **Barbara**, Barb, Barbe,
- **Barclay**, Barkley,
- **Barney**, Barnie, Hebrew, Son of Exhortation, Praise to God
- **Barry**, Barrey, Bary, Irish, Marksman, Strong
- **Baxter**, Baker Middle English Provider Industrious
- **Baylie,** Old French, Stewardship, Protector
- **Beatrice**, Bea, Beatricia,
- **Becky**, Becca, Becka,
- **Beldon**, Belden, Old English, From the Beautiful Valley, Sanctified

- **Belinda**, Belynda, Spanish, Lovely, Beauty of Soul
- **Belle**, Bell, Bellina, French, Beautiful, Blessed
- **Benjamin**, Ben,
- **Bennet**, Bennett, English Blessed Walks With God
- **Bennie**, Benny,
- **Benson**, Bensen, English, Son of Ben, Honor of God
- **Benyamin**, Hebrew, Son of My Right Hand, Mighty
- **Bernadette**, Bernadine, French, Courageous, Valiant
- **Bernard**, Barnard,
- **Bernice**, Berenice, Berni,
- **Bernie**, Birnee, Birney,
- **Bertram**, Bartram, Bert Old English, Brilliant, Magnificent
- **Bessie**, Bess, Bessi,
- **Bessy**, English, Oath of God, Loyal
- **Beth Ann**, Bethann, BethAnn,
- **Bethani,** Bethanie,
- **Betsie,** English, Oath of God, Confirmed
- **Betti**, Bettie, English, Oath of God, Reverent
- **Betty**, Bett, Bette, Bette,
- **Bevin**, Bevin Welsh Son of the Young Warrior Youthful
- **Bianca**, Biancha, Bionca,

- **Bill**, (see William)
- **Birdie**, (See Roberta)
- **Blade**, Blayde, Middle English, Knife, Weapon
- **Blaine**, Blain, Blane,
- **Blair**, Blaire, Irish, Field Worker, Diligent
- **Blaise**, Blaize, Blayze,
- **Blake,** Blakelee,
- **Bob**, (see Robert)
- **Bobbie**, Bobbi, American, Foreigner, Stranger
- **Bodin**, French, Messenger/Herald, Ready for Service
- **Bonni,** Bonnita, Bonny, French, Beautiful, Pure in Heart
- **Bonnie**, Bonita, Bonne,
- **Boone**, Boon, Boonie, French, Good, Obedient
- **Boris**, Boriss, Borris, Slavic Warrior, Trusting
- **Bowen**, Bowie, Gaelic, Small, Victorious
- **Boyce**, Boice, Boise,
- **Boyde**, Boid, Scottis, Golden-Haired, Quiet, Spirit
- **Braden**, English, From the Hill, Called of God
- **Braden**, Bradan, Bradin,
- **Bradford**, Brad,

- **Bradin**, Braeden,
- **Bradlee**, Old English, From the Broad, Meadow Joyful
- **Bradley**, Brad, Bradd,
- **Bradon,** English, From the Broad, Clearing Redeemed
- **Bradon**, Braedon,
- **Brady**, Bradey
- **Brady**, Scandinavian, Glacier, Immovable
- **Branddon**, Branden,
- **Brandi**, Brandie, Middle Dutch, Distilled Wine, Filled With Joy
- **Brandin**, Brandyn,
- **Brandon**, Brandan,
- **Brandy**, Brandee,
- **Brannan**, Brannon, Old English, From the Flaming, Hill Fervent
- **Brant**, Brandt, Brannt,
- **Brantley**, Czech, Proud, Focused
- **Braxton**, Braxtun Old English From Brock's Town Faithful
- **Breanna**, Breeana,
- **Breanne**, Breann, BreAnn,
- **Bre-Anne**, Breeann,
- **Breck**, Brec, Brek, Brekk Irish Freckled Approved
- **Brenda**, Brendie, Old Norse Sword, Glory of God
- **Brendan**, Brenden,
- **Brendin**, Brendon,
- **Brennah**, Brennaugh,

- **Brennan**, Brennen,
- **Brenndan**, Irish, Stinking Hair, Devout
- **Brennon**, Irish, Little Raven, Gift of God
- **Brenton**, Brendt, Brent,
- **Brian**, Briant, Brien,
- **Briana**, Briannah,
- **Brianna,** Celtic, Strong, Dependent
- **Bridget**, Bridgete,
- **Bridgett**, Bridgette,
- **Briele**, Brielle, Brieon,
- **Brina**, Breena, Breina,
- **Brindley**, Brinlee, Brinly,
- **Brit**, Brita, Britt, Britte, Swedish, Strong, Prayerful
- **Britaney**, Britani,
- **Britanny**, Britlee, Britley,
- **Britlyn**, Britynn, Britnee,
- **Britney**, Britni, Britnie,
- **Britny**, Brityn, Brittain,
- **Brittanee**, Brittaney,
- **Brittany**, Britain, Britane,
- **Brock**, Broc, Brocke,
- **Broderick**, Broderic,
- **Brodi,** Irish, Canal Builder, God Is My Foundation
- **Brodie**, Brodee, Brodey,
- **Brodric**, Broadrick

- **Brok**, Broque, Old English, Badger, Full of Praise
- **Bronson**, Bronnson,
- **Brook**, Brooke, Brooks,
- **Bruce**, Bruse, Scottish, From the Woods, Dignity
- **Bruno**, Old German, Brown, Rich in God's Grace
- **Bryan**, see Brian
- **Bryant**, Bryen, Bryent,
- **Bryce**, Brice Welsh Responsive Ambitious
- **Brynley**, Old English, Burnt Wood, Sacrifice
- **Burney**, Old German, Brave as a Bear, Wise
- **Burton**, Berton, Burt, Middle English, From the Fortified Town Amply, Supplied

# C

- **Cady**, Cadee, Cadey,
- **Caecilia**, Cece, Cecelia,
- **Caillin**, Calan, Calin,
- **Caitlin**, Caitlan, Caitland,
- **Caitlynn**, Catlin (see also
- **Caley**, Caylee, Cayley,
- **Calhoun**, Scottish, Strong Warrior, Great in Spirit
- **Calista**, Calista, Calysta,
- **Callaghan**, Irish, Saint, Faithful
- **Callee**, Calleigh, Calli,
- **Callie**, Caleigh, Cali,
- **Calvin**, Cal, Latin, Bald, Favored
- **Cambria**, Camberlee,
- **Camden**, Camdan, Old English, From the Winding, Valley Freedom
- **Camelia**, Camella,
- **Cameran**, Camren,
- **Cameron**, Cam,
- **Cami,** Cammi, Cammie,
- **Camilla,** Cammille,
- **Camille**, Camila, Camill,
- **Cammy** (see also Kami), French, Ceremonial Attendant, Helper
- **Campbell**, Cambell, French, Beautiful Field, Consistent
- **Camron**, Kam, Kameron,
- **Canaan**, Caenan,

- **Candace**, Candice,
- **Candi**, Candy, Candyce,
- **Candra**, Candrea,
- **Candria**, Kandra, Latin, Incandescent, Reflection of Christ
- **Cannen**, Canning, Canon
- **Cannon**, Cannan,
- **Canute**, see Knute
- **Cara**, Caragh, Carah,
- **Caraline**, Carolin,
- **Carey**, Caray, Carrey
- **Cari,** Kari, English, Beloved, Redeemed
- **Carianne**, Carena
- **Carissa**,
- **Carita**, Caritta, Karita,
- **Carl,** Carel, Carle, Carlis,
- **Carla**, Carlia, Karla,
- **Carlan**, Carlen, Carlii,
- **Carlana**, Caraena,
- **Carli**, Carlie, Karlee,
- **Carliana**, Karleena,
- **Carlin,** Karilynn, Karolyn, French, Womanly, Filled With Praise
- **Carlina**, Carleena,
- **Carlissa**, Carlisa,
- **Carlos**, Carlo, Karlo,
- **Carlotta**, Karlotta, Italian, Womanly Godly Heroine
- **Carmela**, Carmalla,
- **Carmelia,** Carmella,

- **Carmellina**, Carmelita, Italian, Garden, Natured of God
- **Carmen,** Carmain,
- **Carmielle**, Carmiya,
- **Carmon,** Karman,
- **Carney**, Karney Irish Victorious Preserved
- **Carol**, Carel, Carole,
- **Carolee,** Carolea,
- **Caroleigh** American, Little Beloved, Just
- **Caroline**, Caralin,
- **Carolyn**, Carrolin,
- **Caron,** Carron, Carrone, Welsh, Loving, Witness
- **Carrie**, Carree, Carri,
- **Carrol,** Carrell, Caroll,
- **Carroline**
- **Carroll** (see also Carol), Gaelic, Champion, Steadfast
- **Carry** (see also Carey,
- **Carson**, Carrson, English, Diligent, Loyal
- **Carter**, Cartar, Old English, Driver of a Cart, Privileged
- **Cartrina**, see Katrina
- **Cary**, Caree, Carree,
- **Caryn,** Caren, Carin,
- **Carynn**, (see also Karen,
- **Carys**, Caris, Carris,

- **Caryss,** (see also Karis), Welsh, Loving, Respectful
- **Casandra**, Casandria,
- **Case**, Casie, Casy,
- **Casey**, Cacey, Cacy,
- **Cashmere,** Cashmir,
- **Casimir**, Cachie, Cash,
- **Casondra,** Cassaundra,
- **Casper,** Caspar, Persian, Treasure, Watchful
- **Cassandra**, Casandera,
- **Cassidy**, Cass, Cassady,
- **Catalina**, Catalena,
- **Caterina**, see Katerina
- **Cathy**, Cathee, Cathey,
- **Cato**, Caton (see also
- **Caysee**, Caysey, Caysie,
- **Cecil**, Cecile, Cecill Latin Blind Illuminated
- **Cecilea**, Cecillia, CeeCee Latin Blind Of the Spirit
- **Cecilia,** Cacelia,
- **Cedric**, Cedrec, Cedric,
- **Cedrik**, English, Battle Chieftain. Courageous Defender
- **Celena**, see Selena
- **Chalina**, Chaeena,
- **Chalise**, Chalissa,
- **Challis**, Challisse,
- **Chalmers**, Chalmer,
- **Chalsey,** French, Goblet, Cheerful

- **Chanah**, Chana, Channa, Hebrew, Favor of God, Prayerful
- **Chandelle**, Chandal,
- **Chandler,** Chandan,
- **Chaning**, English, Wise, Obedient
- **Channelle**, Channel,
- **Channing**, Chane,
- **Chantha,** Chantra
- **Chantrea**, Chantria, Cambodian, Moonbeam, Symbol
- **Chapman**, Chapmann, English, Merchant, Wise
- **Chara,** Charah, Hispanic, Rose, Joy
- **Charelle**, Charil, Charyl,
- **Charese**, Charice,
- **Charis,** Charisa,
- **Charise,** Cher, Cherice,
- **Charissa,** Charesa,
- **Charity,** Chaitee, Chariti, English, Benevolent, Compassionate
- **Charlanna,** Charlena,
- **Charleen,** Charlaine,
- **Charlene,** Charline,
- **Charles,** Charle,
- **Charley,** Charlie, English, Manly, Valiant
- **Charlotte**, Charlette,
- **Charlton**, Charleton,
- **Cherie**, Cheri, Cherie
- **Cheryl,** Chereen,

- **Chesney,** Chesnie, Slavic, Peaceful Regal, Servant
- **Chester,** Ches, Cheston,
- **Chiara**, Chiarah, Italian, Clear, Sealed
- **Chickara**, Chickarra,
- **Chiko**, Chikora, Japanese, Pledge, Promise
- **Chistina**, Christeena,
- **Chloe**, Chloee, Cloe,
- **Chrisie,** Chrissey,
- **Chriss**, Christepher,
- **Christen**, Christian,
- **Christen,** Christyn,
- **Christena**, Christiana,
- **Christene,** Chrystine,
- **Christian,** Christiaan,
- **Christiane**, Christiann,
- **Christianna,** Christinna,
- **Christianos**, Christion,
- **Christie,** Christy, Chrys,
- **Christine**, Christeen,
- **Christopher,** Chris,,
- **Chrystal,** Chrystel,
- **Chrystan,** Chrysten,
- **Chrysti,** Chrystie,
- **Chrystin,** Cristan, Cristen,
- **Cindie,** Cindy, Cynda,
- **Cindy**, see Cythia
- **Cissy,** Cissee, American, Blind, Discerning
- **Claire**, Clair, Clara,

- **Clancy**, Clancey, Irish, Red-Haired Fighter, Christlike
- **Clarance**, Clarrance,
- **Clarence**, Clare,
- **Clarinda,** Clarita, French, Brilliant, Shining Light
- **Clarisa,** Clarisse,
- **Clarissa,** Claresa,
- **Clark**, Clarke, Old French, Scholar, Enlightened Spirit
- **Clarrence,** Latin, Victorious, Pure
- **Clarrisa,** Clarissa,
- **Claudell,** Claudio Latin Lame Loved
- **Claudius,** Claude,
- **Claus**, see Klaus
- **Clay,** Clae, English, Malleable Earth, Adaptable
- **Clayborne,** Claeborne Middle English From the Clay Brook Molded by God
- **Clayton**, Clayten Old English From the Clay Estate Molded by God
- **Clemens**, Clement,
- **Clyde**, Clide, Welsh, Loving, Rewarded
- **Clyff**, Old English, From the River's Heights, Vigilant
- **Cobi,** Cobie, Kobe,
- **Coby,** Cobe, Cobey,
- **Coco,** Cocco, Coccoa
- **Codi,** Codie, Kodee,

- **Cody,** Codee, Codey,
- **Colbert**, Culbert English Brilliant Seafarer Anchored in God
- **Colby**, Colbey, Colbi,
- **Coley,** Colee, Colee,
- **Colin,** Colan, Colen,
- **Collette**, Kolette, Kollette
- **Collier**, Collyer, Welsh, Merchant or Miner, Guided of God
- **Conciana,** Concianna,
- **Concieta,** Italian, Pure, Undefiled
- **Coniah**, Coniyah, Hebrew, God-Appointed, Destined
- **Connor**, Conner,
- **Conny**, Konnie, English, Consistent, Unwavering
- **Conrad**, Conrade,
- **Conroy**, Conroye Irish Wise Strong Leader
- **Consuela**, Konsuela, Spanish, Consoling Friend, Compassionate
- **Cooper**, Courper, English, Barrel Maker, Servant
- **Cort**, see Cortney
- **Cortez**, Courtez, Spanish, Conqueror, Valiant
- **Cortne**, Cortnee,
- **Cortney,** Cortni, Cortnie,
- **Corttney,** Court,
- **Corwin,** Corwyn, Latin, Heart's Delight, Brilliant Countenance
- **Cory**, see Corey

- **Corynn**, English, Little, One Trusting
- **Cosby**, Coz, Cozbee,
- **Courtney,** Cort, Cortnay,
- **Cowan,** Cowey, Irish, From the Hillside, Generous
- **Coy,** Coi, Koy, English, From the Woods, Focused
- **Coyle,** Coyel, Irish, Courageous Leader, God's Warrior
- **Cozbi,** Cosbey, Cosbie,
- **Cozbie**, Cozby, Canaanite, Deceiver, Loving
- **Craig,** Cregg, Crieg,
- **Crandell,** Crandall, English, From the Valley, Freedom
- **Crayton**, English, From the Rocky Place, Humble Spirit
- **Creed**, Creedon, Latin, Belief, Power in Faith
- **Cristian**, Cristiano,
- **Cristin** (see also Kristen), English, Follower of Christ, Obedient
- **Cristina,** Cristiona,
- **Cristofer,** Cristopher,
- **Criston**, Khristian, Kristar,
- **Crosby,** Crosbie, Scandinavian, Shrine of the Cross, Reminder of Christ
- **Crystall**, Crystallin,
- **Curtis**, Curt, Curtiss,

- **Cyndie,** Cyndy Greek Moon Celestial Light
- **Cynthia,** Cindee, Cindi,
- **Cypriana,** Cyprianna,
- **Cyprianne,** Greek, From Cyprus, Bold Witness
- **Cyril,** Cyrill, Cyrille, Greek, Lordly, Great Spiritual Potential
- **Cyrus,** Cy, Cyris Persian Sun Spiritual Enlightenment

# D

- **Daaina**, Dalina, German, Noble Protector, Example
- **Dacey,** Dacee, Daci,
- **Dacia,** Dacia, Latin, Southerner, Divine, Perspective
- **Dacian,** Dacien, Latin, Southerner, Divine Perspective
- **Dacie**, Dacy, Daicee,
- **Daelin**, Dalian, Daylan,
- **Daevon,** Davohn, Davon,
- **Dagan,** Dagon, Hebrew, Grain, Wise
- **Dagana**, Dagania,
- **Daisy**, Daisee, Old German, Vision of the Day, Cleansed
- **Dajuan,** Dawan, Dawon,
- **Dakota,** Dakotah, Sioux Friend, Sincere
- **Dalayna**, Dalena, Dalina,
- **Dale,** Dayle, Old English, From Valley, Peaceful
- **Dallan,** Daelan, Daelen,
- **Dalton,** Dalten, Old English, From the Valley Town, Filled With Peace

- **Daly,** Dalten, Irish, Assembly, Bringer of Light
- **Daman**, Damen,
- **Damara,** Damarrah Czech Glory of the Day Promised Result
- **Damaris,** Damarius,
- **Damarys,** Demaras,
- **Dameon,** Damian,
- **Dametra,** Spanish, Noble Lady, Gracious Spirit
- **Damian,** Daemien,
- **Damiana,** Damianna, Greek, Soother, Healer
- **Damica,** Damika,
- **Damien,** Damion,
- **Damon,** Daemon,
- **Damonn,** Daymon, Greek, Loyal, Walks With God
- **Dana,** Daina, Danah,
- **Danae**, Danay, Dannae
- **Dandrae**, Dandray,
- **Dandre,** De Andre,
- **Dane,** Daine, Dayne,
- **Danell,** Dannell
- **Danelle,** French, God Is My Judge, Perceptive
- **Danelle**, Danel, Danele,
- **Danen,** Danon, American, God Is My Judge, Preserved
- **Danette**, Danett, American, God Is My Judge, Perceptive
- **Dania,** Danee, Dani,

- **Daniah,** Danie, Danni,
- **Danica,** Daneeka,
- **Daniel,** Dan, Daniyel,
- **Daniela,** Daniele, Daniell,
- **Daniella**, Dannielle,
- **Danielle**, French, God Is My Judge, Discerning
- **Danielle,** Danialle,
- **Danika,** Dannika Slavic Morning Star Attentive
- **Dannon,** Danaan,
- **Danny,** Donyel, Donyell, Hebrew, God Is My Judge, Discerning
- **Dante,** Dauntay,
- **Danya**, Hebrew, God Is My Judge, Intuitive
- **Danya,** Danyah, Donya
- **Danyel,** Danyele,
- **Daphne,** Daphaney,
- **Darbie**, Irish, Freedom, Free Spirit
- **Darby,** Darbey, Darbi,
- **Darcie,** Darcy, Darsey,
- **Darcy**, Darcee, Darcey,
- **Daria,** Darria, Darya, Greek, Wealthy, Gracious
- **Darias**, Darien, Darion Persian Prosperous Preserved
- **Darielle**, Dariel, Darriel,
- **Darin**, Darran, Darrian,
- **Darius,** Darian, Dariann,

- **Darlene**, Darla, Darleen,
- **Darling,** French, Darling, Loving
- **Darnall,** Darnell, Irish, Magnificent, Loving
- **Darnelle,** Darnall,
- **Daron,** Darius, Deron, Irish, Great, Esteemed
- **Daron,** Darren, Welsh, Freedom, Spirit-Filled
- **Daron,** Darron, Daryn,
- **Darrah,** Hebrew, Compassionate, Bearer of Mercy
- **Darral,** Darrel, Darril,
- **Darrell,** Darelle, Daril,
- **Darren,** Daran, Daren,
- **Darren,** Darius, Deron, English, Rocky Hill, Obedient
- **Darrick**, Darrik, Dereck,
- **Darrielle**, French, Little Darling, Cherished
- **Darrien**, Darrin, Deren,
- **Darryl,** Darryll, Daryl,
- **Darsie**, French, Fortress, Established in Strength
- **Darwin,** Darwyn, Old English, Beloved, Treasured
- **Darynn,** Darynne,
- **Dasan**, Dassan, Pomo Leader, Chosen
- **Dasha,** Dashah, Dasya, Russian, Divine, Display Miracle,
- **Daveena**, Davi, Daviana,

- **David,** Dave, Daved,
- **Davin**, Daevin, Daevon,
- **Davina,** Davina, Dava,
- **Davine**, Davinia, Davira,
- **Davis,** Davidson, Davies,
- **Davison**, English, Honorable, Loving
- **Davon,** English, From Devonshire, Obedient
- **Davonn,** Davontay,
- **Davonte**, Dayvin,
- **Dawn,** Dawnan, Dawna,
- **Dawne,** Dawnn, Dawnna,
- **Dawnya,** Danya,
- **Dawson,** Dawsen, English, Son of the Beloved, Victorious
- **Daya**, Daeya, Daia, Hebrew, Bird, Secure
- **Dayana**, Dayahna, Middle Eastern, Divine, Warrior
- **Daycee**, Daycie, Gaelic, Southerner, Friend of Christ
- **Daylen,** Daylin, English, From the Dale, Secure
- **Daymian**, Russian, Soother, One Who Restores
- **Dayna,** Daynah, Scandinavian, Bright as Day, Obedient
- **Daythan,** Daython, Hebrew, Belonging to the Law, Redeemed

- **Dayvid,** Hebrew, Beloved, Lover of All
- **Deacon,** Deke, Diakonos, Greek, One Who Serves, Honored
- **Dean,** Deane, Dene, Old English, Valley, Prosperous
- **Deandra,** Deandrea,
- **Deandre,** D'Andre,
- **Deandria,** Deanndra,
- **Deanna,** Deana, Deann,
- **Deanne**, Deeann,
- **Deaundre,** Deondre, French, Courageous, Submissive
- **Debbi**, Debbie, Debbora,
- **Debborah,** Debby, Debi,
- **Debora**, Debora,
- **Deborrah,** Debra, Hebrew, Honey Bee, New Era of Leadership
- **Dedrick,** Detrick, Didrik,
- **Dee**, Dede, Deedee Welsh Dark Loving
- **Deeanna,** Latin, Divine, Brightness of the Dawn
- **Deena,** see Dena
- **Deidra,** Deidre, Dierdra,
- **Deimas,** Greek, Ruler of People, Powerful
- **Deirdre**, Dedra, Deedra,
- **Deitra,** Deetra, Detria, Greek, Abundant, Refreshed

- **Deja,** Daija, Daja, French, Before, Compassionate
- **Dejuan,** Dewaun, Dijuan,
- **Dejuan**, see Dejuan
- **Delaiah**, Dalaiah, Hebrew, God Is the Deliverer, Redeemed
- **Delainey**, Delanny,
- **Delana**, Dalanna,
- **Delano**, Dellano, French, Nut Tree, Anchored
- **Delany,** Dalaney,
- **Delaynie,** Dellaney, Irish, Of the Champion, Victorious
- **Delbert**, English, Bright as Day, Obedient
- **Delia**, Dehlia, Deleah,
- **Delicia**, Deleesha,
- **Delisha,** Delysia, Latin, Delightful, Joyous Spirit
- **Della,** Dellie, Old German, Noble Maiden, Excellent Virtue
- **Dellia**, Delya, Greek, Visible, Divine Reflection
- **Delmar**, Dalmar, Latin, By the Sea, Filled With Praise
- **Delores,** Deloria, Deloris,
- **Delsie**, Delcee, Delsee, English, Oath of God, Promise
- **Delta,** Greek, Door, Seeker of Truth

- **Demario,** Italian, Son of a Warrior, Seed of a Righteous Soldier
- **Demaris,** Demarius, Greek, Gentle, Forgiven
- **Demas,** Deemas,
- **Demetra**, Demitra, Greek, Plentiful, Fruitful
- **Demetreaus,** Demetrias,
- **Demetreus,**
- **Demetri**, Dimitrie, Dmitri,
- **Demetria,**
- **Demetric,** Demetrik,
- **Demetrius,** Russian, Immeasurable, Gracious
- **Demica,** Demicah, French, Friendly, Seeker of Truth
- **Demitrik**, Demitrias
- **Dempsey**, Dempsie, Irish, Proud, Honorable
- **Dena**, Deena, Native American, From the Valley, Peaceful
- **Denae,** Denay, Denee
- **Denham,** Denhem, English, From the Valley Village, One of Integrity
- **Denice**, Deniece,
- **Denise**, Danice, Deni,
- **Dennis**, Dennes, Denny, Greek, Happy, Effective
- **Dennise**, French, Favored, Reborn

- **Dennzel**, Denzell, Denzil, English, From Cornwall,
- **Denton,** Dentin, English, From a Happy Home, Trusting Spirit
- **Denzel,** Danzel, Danzell,
- **Deon,** Deion, Deone,
- **Deonna,** Deonne, Dione,
- **Deontee,** Deontre, Dion,
- **Derek,** Darek, Darik,
- **Dericka**, Derrica, Derrika, German, Ruler of the People, Gifted
- **Derika,** Dereka, Derica,
- **Desiree,** Desarae,
- **Desmon,** Desmund,
- **Devin,** Devan, Deven,
- **Devine,** Devyn, Irish, Poet, Seeker of Wisdom
- **Devon**, Devonlee,
- **Devona,** Devonda,
- **Devoney,** Devony, Gaelic, Dark-Haired, Sacrifice
- **Dewey,** Dewie, Welsh, Prized, Prosperous
- **Dexter**, Dextor, Latin, Skilled in Workmanship, Industrious
- **Dezirae**, Deziree, French, Desired, Likeness of God
- **Dezmond,** Irish, Youthful, Refreshing

- **Dhane**, Old English, Trickling, Stream Blessed
- **Di,** Diahann, Dianah,
- **Diamond,** Diamonique,
- **Diamonte,** Latin, Precious Gem, Carefully Guarded
- **Diana,** Daiana, Daianna,
- **Dick**, Dic, Dickenson,
- **Diedrick**, German, Ruler of the People, Respected
- **Diego,** Diaz, Spanish, Supplanter, Wise
- **Dierdre**, Irish, Wanderer, Seeker of Righteousness and Truth
- **Dacian**, Dalbert, Del,
- **Dillin** (see also Dylan), Irish, Faithful, Steadfast in Christ
- **Dillon**, Dillan, Dillen,
- **Dimitri**, Greek, Lover of the Earth, Fruitful Increase
- **Dimitri,** Demitre,
- **Dimitrios**, Dimitrius,
- **Dinah**, Dina, Dyna,
- **Dino,** Deeno, German, Little Sword, Covenant
- **Dion,** see Deon
- **Dixie**, Dixee, Dixi, Dixy, French, Tenth, Blessing
- **Dixon,** Dickson, English, Son of the Ruler, Youthful Courage
- **D'Juan,** Dujuan, American, God Is Gracious, Promise

- **Dmetrius**
- **Dolan,** Dolin, Dolyn, Irish, Dark-Haired, Full of Life
- **Dollie**, American, Compassionate, Christlike
- **Dolly**, Dollee, Dolli,
- **Dolores**, Spanish, Sorrowful, Compassionate
- **Dolph**, Dolf, Slavic, Famous, Great
- **Domenico**, Domenick,
- **Dominika**, Latin, Belonging to the Lord, Consecrated
- **Dominique,** Dominica,
- **Donald,** Don, Donn,
- **Donata**, Donatta, Latin, Gift of God, Contemplative
- **Donna,** Old English, Beginning Anew, Joy and Praise
- **Donovan**, Donavan,
- **Dora,** Doralia, Doralie, Greek, Gift of God, Wise
- **Doran,** Dorin, Doron,
- **Dorcas**, Greek, Filled With Grace, Heir
- **Doreen,** Dorene, Dorey,
- **Dori**, Dorie, Dorrie,
- **Dorian**, Doriana,
- **Doriann**, Dorianna,
- **Dorien**, Dorion, Dorrian,
- **Doris**, Dorice, Dorise,

- **Dorothea**, Dorothee,
- **Dorothy,** Dottie, Dotti,
- **Dorran**, Dorren, Hebrew, God's Gift, Sacrifice
- **Douglas**, Doug,
- **Douglass**, Scottish, From the Dark Stream, Adventurous
- **Doyle**, Doyal, Irish, Dark Stranger, Guided by the Spirit
- **Drake**, Drago, Latin, Dragon, Symbol
- **Drew,** Drewe, Dru, Drue, Welsh, Wise, Esteemed
- **Drisana**, Drisanna, Sanskrit, Daughter of the Sun, Loyal
- **Duncan,** Duncon, Scottish, Steadfast Warrior, Strong in Faith
- **Dunstan,** Dunsten, English, From the Stony Hill, Victorious
- **Durant,** Durand,
- **Dustin**, Dustan, Dusten,
- **Duston**, Dusty, Dustyn, German, Valiant Warrior, Brave
- **Dwayne**, DeWayne,
- **Dwight**, Dwieght, English, Fair, Diligent Leader
- **Dyana**, Dyane, Dyann,
- **Dyanna**, Dyanne, Latin, Divine, Glorious
- **Dylan**, Dyllan, Dyllon,
- **Dylana**, Dylanna, Welsh, From the Sea, Devoted

- **Dylon** (see also Dillon), Welsh, From the Sea, Resolute Courage
- **Dynah**, Hebrew, God Has Vindicated, Righteous

# E

- **Elainna**, Elani, Elania,
- **Eladah**, Eilada, Elada,
- **Elden**, Eldin, Old English, Wise, Guardian, Good Judgment
- **Ephron**, Hebrew, Strong, Thankful
- **Emilyann,** Emilyanne, American, Gracious, Thoughtful
- **Emmet**, Emitt, Emmett,
- **Emilio**, Emillio, Italian, Glorifier, Obedient
- **Enrique,** Enrico, Enrikos,
- **Estelita,** Estella, Estrela,
- **Eliora**, Eliaura, Eliorra,
- **Everette**, Everitt, German, Courageous, Unending Praise
- **Elynn,** Elinn, Elyne,
- **Earl**, Earle, English, Noble, Reflected Image
- **Emily,** Emalee, Emelie,
- **Emilian**, Emille, Emils, Polish, Eager, Purified
- **Edana**, Edanna, Edena, Irish, Ardent Flame, Unending Love
- **Easter**, Eastre, Old German, Spring Festival, Celebration
- **Ethan,** Eathan, Ethen,
- **Ennis,** Enis

- **Eliah,** Eliyah, Hebrew, The Lord Is God, Believer
- **Eugene,** Gene, Greek, Born to Nobility, Vivacious
- **Ellise**, Ellyce, Ellyse,
- **Erica**, Arica, Aricka,
- **Emanuell,** Emmanuel,
- **Edmund,** Edmon,
- **Elaine,** Elain, Elane,
- **Ember,** Embur (see also
- **Egan,** Eagan, Egann,
- **Elisabethe**, Hebrew, Oath of God, Consecrated
- **Elvis,** Elvys, Old Norse, All-Wise, Righteous
- **Emmelie**, Emylee
- **Emanuel**, Emanual,
- **Eira**, Eirah, Welsh, Snow, Pure
- **Elise**, Elisse, Ellice,
- **Edward**, Ed, Eddie,
- **Emery**, Emeri, Emmery,
- **Eirenna**, English, Peace, Contentment
- **Enrique**, Spanish, Head of the Household, Servant
- **Emerson,** Emmerson, English, Son of the Leader, Victorious
- **Elana**, Elaina, Elaina,
- **Eyota,** Eyotah, Native American, Greatest, Servant

- **Elias,** Ellis, Greek, God Is My Salvation, Mouthpiece of God
- **Eden,** Eaden, Eadin,
- **Elgin**, Elgen, English, Noble, Responsible
- **Elijah**, Elija, Eliyahu, Hebrew, The Lord Is My God, Spiritual Champion
- **Evin,** Evyn, Irish, Young Warrior, Noble Protector
- **Edith,** Edythe, Old English, Valuable, Gift Wise
- **Eryka**, Erykka, Old Norse, Brave, Victorious
- **Elva,** Elvia
- **Eriq,** Erric, Errick, Errick,
- **Erikka,** Errica, Errika,
- **Eleanor,** Eleanore,
- **Etienne**, Etiene, French, Enthroned, Humble
- **Erinne**, Erin, Eryn, Erynn,
- **Erhard**, Erhardt, Erhart, German, Resolute, Efficient
- **Erwin**, see Irwin
- **Evelyn**, Evalina, Evaline,
- **Ellynn**, American, Clear Pool, Cleansed
- **Estrella**, Estelina,
- **Edwin**, Edwyn, Edwina, Old English, Prosperous Friend, Belonging to God
- **Ernst**, English, Sincere, Free in Spirit
- **Edmond**, Edmonde,

- **Estelle**, Estele, French, Star, Infinite Potential
- **Eythan**, Hebrew, Firmness, Steadfast in Truth
- **Eldon,** Elldon, English, From the Holy Hill, Enlightened
- **Elliot,** Eliot, Eliott, Elliott, Hebrew, The Lord Is My God, Consecrated
- **Esau**, Esaw, Hebrew, Hairy Strength
- **Ellis**, see Elias
- **Eldridge**, Eldredge, German, Mature Counselor, Godly
- **Ellen**, Elen, Ellan, Ellin, English, Bright Heir
- **Edna**, Ednah, Hebrew, Rejuvenated, Filled With Pleasure
- **Edgar,** Ed, English, Prosperous, Gifted
- **Esmond** Old English, Blessed, Peace, Prosperous Protector
- **Everlee,** Everleigh, English, From the Boar Meadow, Faithful
- **Emmi,** Emmie, English, Striving, Attentive
- **Ezra**, Esera, Esra, Ezera,
- **Edin**, Edyn, Hebrew, Delightful, Pleasing
- **Emma,** Ema, Old German, All-Embracing, Absolute Faith
- **Estee,** English, Star, Fulfillment

- **Ellie**, Elie, Elli, Estonian, Illuminated, Shining Light
- **Emil**, Emill, German, Industrious, Diligent Seeker
- **Einar**, Ejnar, Old Norse, Individualist, Free
- **Elan,** Elann
- **Elasya**, Hebrew, God Has Created, Image of God
- **Eric**, Aric, Arik, Arick,
- **Ernest**, Ernesto, Ernie,
- **Electra,** Elektra, Greek, Brilliant, Eternal Hope
- **Ella**, Ellah, Old German, Beautiful, Sustained
- **Eli**, Ely, Hebrew, Uplifted, Delivered
- **Elton,** Alten, Alton, Ellton, English, From the Old Town, Steadfast
- **Emerald,** Emeralde, French, Green Gem, Breathtaking
- **Elinor,** Ellenora, Elynora, Greek, Bright as the Sun, Kindhearted
- **Emelia**, Amilia, Emalia,
- **Easton**, Eason, English, From the Eastern Town, Christlike
- **Elissa,** Lissa, Latin, Sweetly Blissful, Strong Faith
- **Elizabeth**, Elisabeth,
- **Enrica**, Enrikka, French, Home Ruler, Righteous
- **Emery,** Turkish, Brother God's, Servant

- **Emilie**, Emillie, Emilly,
- **Emiliann**, Emilianne,
- **Esmunde**, Old English, Rich Protector, Gracious
- **Emmy**, Emee, Emi,
- **Ellissa,** Ellisia, Ellyssa,
- **Evelynne**, English, Hazelnut, Radiant
- **Ethel**, Ethyl, Old English, One of High Regard, Noble
- **Erin**, Erine, Erinn,
- **Ellison,** Elison, Ellyson, English, Son of the Redeemed, One Near to God's Heart
- **Eve,** Eva, Evah, Evie, Hebrew, Mother of Life, Full of Life
- **Eda**, Edah, Irish, Loyal, Faithful
- **Emmott**, Old English, Earnest, Genuine, Devotion
- **Elvira**, Elvera, Spanish, Fair, Wise
- **Emile**, Emilee, Emiley,
- **Ebonee,** Eboney, Ebonie, American, Hard, Dark Wood Shining
- **Elysa,** Elyssa
- **Evita**, Eveeta, Hispanic, Youthful Life, Childlike
- **Esme,** Esmee, French, Overcomer, Victor
- **Eleena**, Elina, Ellena, Russian, Radiant, Illuminated
- **Eddy,** Eduardo, Edwardo,

- **Eagan,** see Egan
- **Elisha**, Elishah, Elishia,
- **Enos,** Enosh, Hebrew, Man, Expectant
- **Evangeline,** Evangelina, Greek, Bringer of Good News, Happy Messenger
- **Emily,** Latin, Industrious, Blessed
- **Elissa**, Elisia, Ellisa,
- **Emilianna**, Emiliana,
- **Eunice**, Eunique, Eunise, Greek, Joyous, Victorious

# F

- **Fabia**, Fabiana,
- **Fabian,** Fabayan,
- **Fabianna**, Fabianne,
- **Fabiano**, Fabien, Fabio,
- **Fabria**, Fabriana,
- **Falina**, Falena, Faylina,
- **Falyn,** Irish, Grandchild of the Ruler, Heir
- **Fannie**, English, French, Dedicated
- **Fanny,** Fanney, Fanni,
- **Fanya,** Fania, Fannia, Russian, Free, Vindicated
- **Farron**, Farryn, Faryn
- **Felecia**, Felicya,
- **Felicity,** Felicianna,
- **Felina**, Latin, Catlike, Upright
- **Felipe**, see Phillip
- **Felisha,** Latin, Fortunate, Joyful
- **Felissa,** Feliza, Felysse, English, Joyful, Content
- **Felix**, see Phillip, Latin, Fortunate, Blessed
- **Felton**, Felten, English, From the Field Town, Hopeful

- **Fenton,** Fenny, English, From the Marshland, Spirit of Life
- **Ferdinand**, Ferdnand, Gothic Adventurous, Seeker of Truth
- **Ferell,** Ferryl, Irish, Valiant, Servant
- **Feris**, Middle Eastern, Horseman, Fearsome
- **Finian**, Phinean, Irish, Fair Hero, Servant
- **Fiona,** Fionna, Irish, Fair, Persevering
- **Fletcher**, Flecher, Fletch Anglo-Saxon Arrow Featherer, Ingenious
- **Flora,** Floria, Floriana,
- **Florann**, Floren, Florida,
- **Florence**, Flo, Florance,
- **Florian**, Florien, Florrian, English, Blooming, Nourished
- **Florianna**, Latin, Flower, Nurtured
- **Florrie**, Flossie, Latin, Flourishing, Prosperous
- **Floyd**, Floydd, Welsh, White-or-Gray-Haired, Wise
- **Flynn**, Flinn, Flyn, Gaelic, Son of Redhead, Blessed
- **Fontana**, French, Fountain, Sustained
- **Fontanna,** Fontaine,
- Forbes, Forbe Gaelic Prosperous Blessed
- **Forrest,** Forest, Forster,

- **Frazer**, Frazier, French, Strawberry, Filled With Life
- **Frederica**, Freddi,
- **Frederick**, German, Peaceful Ruler, Perceptive
- **Fredericka**, Frederina,
- **Frederique**, Fredrika, Old German, Peaceful Ruler, Compassionate
- **Freia,** Frieda, German, Serene, Victorious
- **Freida**, Freda, Freeda,
- **Freja**, Fraya, Freya, Swedish, Virtuous, Woman Valuable

# G

- **Gabriala**, Gabralla,
- **Gabriana,** Gabrianna,
- **Gabriel,** Gab, Gabe,
- **Gabriela**, Gabriele,
- **Gabriell**, Gabrielli,
- **Gabriella,** Hebrew, Devoted to God, Confident
- **Gabrielle,** Gabbey,
- **Gabriello**, Gibbbee,
- **Galiena,** Galienna, Old German, Supreme, Respectful
- **Galina,** Gailina, Russian, Shining, Glorified
- **Galvin**, Galvan, Galven, Gaelic, Glowing, Blessed
- **Gannen**, Irish, White, Devout
- **Gannon**, Gannan,
- **Ganya**, Gania, Ganyah, Hebrew. Garden of God, Refreshed
- **Gareth,** Garith, Garreth Welsh Gentle Peaceful
- **Garner**, Garnier French Guard One of Integrity
- **Garvin**, Garvan, Garvyn, English, Friend in Battle, Peaceful

- **Gary**, Garry, German, Mighty, Regenerated
- **Gaston**, Gascon, Gaston, French, From Gascony, Protected
- **Gavin**, Gavan, Gaven,
- **Gavyn**, Welsh, White Hawk, Content
- **Gayle**, Old English, My Father, Rejoices, Lively
- **Geary,** Gearey, English, Changeable, Courageous
- **Geffrey**, Geoff, Geoffrey,
- **Gemina,** Gemmina Greek Twin Righteous
- **Gemini**, Gemelle,
- **Gena**, see Gina
- **Gene,** see Eugene
- **Geneen**, see Jeanine
- **Geneva**, Jeneva, French, Juniper Tree, Wise
- **Genevieve**, Genavieve,
- **Genna**, see Jenna
- **Gennifer,** see Jennifer
- **Geoffrey**, Geffery,
- **George,** Georges,
- **Georgeanna**, Georgene,
- Gerald, Geraldo,
- **Geraldine**, Geraldina,
- **Gerrett** (Jarrett), Irish, Warrior, Free
- **Gerry**, Jeraldine, Old German, Powerful, Victorious

- **Gianna**, Gianna,
- **Gibbie,** Hebrew, Devoted to God, Brave
- **Gibson,** Gilson, English, Son of the Honest Man, Fruitful
- **Gilbert,** Gibb, Gibbs, Gil,
- **Gilda,** Gilde, Anglo-Saxon, Covered With Gold, Blessed
- **Gillian**, see Jillian
- **Gilmore**, Gilmour, Irish, Devout, Dependent
- **Gina**, Geena, Gena,
- **Ginah**, Ginia (see also
- **Ginny,** Gini, Ginni,
- **Gino**, Geno, Greek, Of Noteworthy Birth, Delivered
- **Gizelle,** Gissele, Giselle,
- **Gladys**, Gladis, Irish, Princess, Spiritual Understanding
- **Glendon,** Glenden, Scottish, From the Valley Fortress, Excellent Worth
- **Glenna**, Glenda, Irish, From The Valley, Blooming
- **Gloria,** Gloriela,
- **Gloriella**, Glorielle, Glory,
- **Godfrey**, Godfry
- **Gordon**, Gordan,
- **Grace**, Gracey, Graci,
- **Gracia**, Graciana, Gracie, Latin, Patient, Full of Grace
- **Grady,** Gradey, Gaelic, Noble, Strong

- **Grant**, Grantham,
- **Grayson**, Greyson, Middle Eastern, Son of the Bailiff, One of Knowledge
- **Greggory**, Gregori, Greig,
- **Gregory**, Greg, Gregg,
- **Gresham**, Grisham English From the Village by the Pasture Peaceful
- **Gustaf**, Gustav,
- **Gustave**, Gus, Guss,
- **Gustavus,** Scandinavian, God's Staff, Blessed

*H*

- **Hal**, see Harold
- **Halen**, Haylan, Swedish, Hall, Gracious
- **Halena,** Helana,
- **Haley,** Halley, Halli, Hally, Nigerian, Unexpected Gift, Blessing
- **Hamilton**, Hamelton, Old English, From the Fortified Castle, Faithful
- **Hamlet,** Hamlett, Old Norse, From the Village, Compassionate
- **Hana**, Hanita, Japanese, Flower, Joyful
- **Hanan**, Hannan,
- **Haniel**, Hanniel, Hebrew, Grace of God, Restored
- **Hannah**, Hanna, Hebrew, Gracious, Compassionate
- **Hannen**, Hannon, Hebrew, Merciful, Compassionate
- **Hardin**, Hardan, English, From the Hares' Valley, Righteous
- **Hardy**, English, Bold, Confident
- **Harley,** Harlee, Harleigh, Old English, From the Rabbit Pasture, Chosen of God

- **Harmonie**, Latin, Oneness, Unifier
- **Harmony,** Harmoni,
- **Harold**, Hal, Herald,
- **Harper,** Harpo, English, Harp Player, Instrument of Praise
- **Harriet**, Harriett, Hattie, Old German, Ruler of the Household, Discerner of Excellence
- **Harris**, Harrison, Old English, Son of the Strong Man, Courageous
- **Harry**, Harray, Harrey, Old German, Home Ruler, Integrity
- **Hartley**, Hartlee,
- **Harvey**, French, Warrior, Steadfast
- **Harvey**, Harv
- **Haven,** Havan, Havin, Dutch, Harbor, Preserved
- **Hayden,** Haden, Haydn,
- **Haydon** (see also
- **Hayes**, Hays, English, From the Hedged Valley, Moderate
- **Haywood,** Heywood, English, From the Hedged, Forest Chosen
- **Heath**, Heathe, English, Shrub, Protector
- **Heather,** Heatherlee, Middle English, Flowering, Blooming Cover of Beauty

- **Hector,** Hectar, Greek, Steadfast, One of Integrity
- **Heidi**, Heide, Heidee,
- **Heinrich**, Heinrick,
- **Helen,** Hellen, Greek, Light, Righteous
- **Helena**, Haleena,
- **Henley**, see Hanley
- **Henrietta**, Henrieta, English, Household Ruler, Strong
- **Henry,** Hank, Henri,
- **Hensley**, English, From the High Pasture Protector, Shepard
- **Hercules**, Greek, Glorious, Gift Enduring
- **Herick**, Herrik, German, War Ruler, Chosen
- **Herman,** Hermann,
- **Hilary,** Hillaree, Hillarie,
- **Hilda**, Hilde, Old German, Battle Maid, Courageous
- **Hillary,** Hilaree, Hilari,
- **Hilleree**, Hillory, English, Cheerful, Blessed
- **Hilton**, Hillton, English, From the Hill Town, Obedient
- **Hogan**, Hogen, Gaelic, Youthful, Generous
- **Holbrook**, Holbrooke, Old English, From the Brook, Peaceful
- **Holden,** Holdin English From the Valley Hollow Fearless

- **Holli**, Hollie, Old English, Holly Tree, Peaceful
- **Hollis**, Hollyss, Old English, From the Holly Trees, Righteous
- **Holly**, Hollee, Holley,
- **Hollyann**, Hollianna,
- **Hope**, Hopie, Old English, Trust in the Future, Understanding Heart
- **Howard,** Howie English Chief Guardian Discerning
- **Howel**l, Howel Welsh Remarkable Reconciled
- **Hugh**, Huey, Hughes,
- **Hugo**, Old German, Thoughtful, Wise

# I

- **Ian**, Ean, Iain, Scottish, God Is Gracious, Discreet
- **Ianos**, Iano, Ianos, Czech, God Is Gracious, Divine Vision
- **Ida,** Idaleena, Idarina, German, Youth, Industrious
- **Idalia,** Idalis, Idalys, American, Creative, Gifted
- **Ilan**, Illan, Hebrew, Youth, Pride of the Father
- **Ilana**, Ilani, Illana,
- **Iliana**, Ileana, Illiana
- **Illanda,** Illani, Hebrew, Tree, Firmly Rooted
- **Ilona,** Ileena, Ilina, Hungarian, Light, Disciple of Christ
- **Ilya,** Ilias, Iljah
- **Iman,** Imani, Middle Eastern, Believer, Illuminated
- **Imelda**, Imalda, Swiss, All-Encompassing, Battle Victorious
- **Imla,** Imlah, Hebrew, Fulfilling, Prosperous
- **Immanuel**, Immanuela,
- **Ina,** Inah, Irish, Pure, Divine Inspiration

- **India**, Indya, English, From India, Gift of Faith
- **Ingemar,** Ingeborg, Old Norse, Famous Son, Adventurous
- **Inger,** Ing, Inga, Inge, Old Norse, Army of the Son, Kind
- **Ingerlisa**, Ingerlise, Norwegian, Praised Daughter, Consecrated to God
- **Ingram,** Ingraham,
- **Ingrid,** Ingela, Old Norse, Hero's Daughter, Cherished
- **Ingrim**, Old Norse, King's Raven, Wise
- **Ioan**, Ioann, Romanian, God Is Gracious, Cherished
- **Ioanna**, Ioana, Russian, God Is Gracious, Set Apart
- **Iola,** Iolia, Greek, Dawn of Day, One Made Worthy
- **Iolana,** Ioanna, Hawaiian, Soaring Like a Hawk, Steadfast
- **Iona,** Ione, Ionia, Greek, Violet Flower, Inner Beauty
- **Ira,** Irah Hebrew Watchful Led by the Spirit
- **Irina,** Irana, Iriana,
- **Iris,** Irisa, Irisha, Irissa,
- **Irving**, Earvin, Erv,
- **Irwin**, Erwin, Erwyn,

- **Irwyn** Old English, Friend, Triumphant Spirit
- **Isaac**, Ike, Isaak, Isac,
- **Isabel,** Isabela, Isabella,
- **Isabelle**, Izabel, Izabele,
- **Isadora**, Isidora, Isidora, Greek, Gift of the Goddess, Inspired
- **Isaiah**, Ishmael, Ishmeil,
- **Isak**, Ishaq, Itzak, Izaac,
- **Ivan,** Iven, Russian, God Is Gracious, Triumphant
- **Ivana**, Ivania, Ivanna, Slavic, God Is Gracious, Thankful
- **Ivar**, Iver, Ivor, Old Norse, Noble, Peaceful
- **Ivonne,** Ivette, Ivete,
- **Ivory,** Ivori, American, Made of Ivory, Fearless
- **Ivy,** Ivey, Ivie, English, Ivy Plant, Trusting
- **Iwan,** Iwann Polish God Is Gracious Grateful
- **Izaak,** Izac, Izak, Izakk,
- **Izabelle,** Spanish, Consecrated to God, Discerning Spirit
- **Izzy,** Yitzak, Yitzhak, Hebrew, Laughter, Child of Promise

*J*

- **Jacey**, J.C., Jace, Jacee,
- **Jack**, Jackie, Jacky, Jax, English, God Is Gracious, Redeemed
- **Jackee**, Jacki, Jacklyn,
- **Jackson**, Jakson, Jaxon, English, Son of Jack, Gracious
- **Jacob,** Jacobb, Jacobs,
- **Jacobi**, Jackobi, Scottish, Replacement, Joyous
- **Jacon** (see also Jaakan), Hebrew, Trouble, Victorious
- **Jacqueline,** Jacalyn,
- **Jacquelyn**, Jacquelynn,
- **Jacques,** Jacquan,
- **Jacy**, Jaicy
- **Jada**, Jaeda, Jaida,
- **Jade,** Jadah, Jadi, Jadie,
- **Jadon,** Jaden, Jadin,
- **Jady,** Jaide, Jayde, Spanish, Precious Gem, Priceless
- **Jael,** Jaela, Jaelle (see
- **Jaelynn,** Jalen, Jalin,
- **Jaime**, Jaimey, Jaimee,
- **Jaison,** Jasan, Jasen,
- **Jake**, Jayke, English, Substitute, New Covenant

+ **Jamelia**, Jamelle,
+ **Jamelya**, Jamilia,
+ **James**, Jaimes, Jaymes,
+ **Jameson**, Jamerson,
+ **Jami**, Jamia, Jamian,
+ **Jamian**, Jamiel, Jaymin, Hebrew, Favored, Triumphant
+ **Jamie,** Jamee, Jamey,
+ **Jamiel,** Jamil, Jamill,
+ **Jamii,** Jammie, Jamya,
+ **Jamila,** Jahmela,
+ **Jamilla**, Yamila, Middle Eastern, Beautiful, Loving
+ **Jan**, Jani, Jania, Jann German God's Gift Cherished
+ **Jana**, Janna (see also
+ **Janae,** Janaya, Janaya,
+ **Janan**, Janani, Janann, Middle Eastern, Tenderhearted, Gentle
+ **Jane**, Jaine, Janet,
+ **Janea**, Janay, Jannay,
+ **Janell,** Janella, Janiel,
+ **Janelle**, Janel, Janele,
+ **Janessa,** Janiesha,
+ **Janett,** Janey, Janie,
+ **Janette**, Jannine,
+ **Janice,** Janis, Jannie,
+ **Janielle**, Jannel, Jannell,
+ **Janzen**, Jensen, Scandinavian, Son of Jan, Joyful
+ **Jarell,** Jarel, Jarelle,
+ **Jarvis**, Jarvas, Jarvares,

- **Jasmaine**, Jasman,
- **Jasmin**, Jasmon,
- **Jasmine**, Jas, Jasmain,
- **Jason,** Jacen, Jaeson,
- **Jasper,** Jaspar, English, Treasure Holder, Richly Blessed
- **Jassmine**, Jassmyn, Jaz,
- **Jay,** Jey, Old French, Vivacious, Adventurous
- **Jaya**, Jaea, Jaia, Jayla,
- **Jaycee**, Jaycey, Jaycie
- **Jaycie**, Jaciel, Jayce,
- **Jazmin**, Jazmine,
- **Jeaneen,** Jeanett,
- **Jeanette**, Janeen,
- **Jeanine,** Jeannette,
- **Jeannine,** Jenine, French, God Is Gracious, Preserved
- **Jeffery**, Jeffrie, Jeffries,
- **Jeffrey,** Jefery, Jeff,
- **Jelani,** Jeanee, Jelani,
- **Jenney**, Jennie,
- **Jennifer,** Jen, Jenefer,
- **Jenniffer**, Jenny, Welsh, Fair, Trusting
- **Jeremee**, Jeremey,
- **Jeremia**, Jeremias,
- **Jeremiah**, Jeramiah,
- **Jeremii**, English, God Is Exalted, Humble
- **Jeremy**, Jeramee,

- **Jeroham**, Jeroam, Hebrew, Loved, Treasured
- **Jesse,** Jesee, Jess,
- **Jessica**, Jesi, Jesica,
- **Jessie**, Jessika, Jessy,
- **Jewel**, Jewell, Jewelle, French, Gem, Precious
- **Jilanna**, see Gianna
- **Jilian**, Jiliana, Jiliann,
- **Jilianna**, Jill, Jillana,
- **Jillene**, Jilliana, Jillianne,
- **Jillian,** Gillian, Jil,
- **Jillisa,** Latin, Youthful, Regenerated
- **Jim,** Jimi, Jimmee,
- **Jimelle,** Hebrew, Handsome, Image of God
- **Jimmie**, Jimmy, Jimy, Hebrew, Supplanter, Nurtured
- **Jin,** Jinn, Chinese, Gold, True Worth
- **Jina**, Jinna (see also
- **Jindrich**, Jindrick, Czech, Head of the Household, Trusted
- **Jinny**, see Ginny
- **Jiovanni,** Jovaan, Jovani,
- **Joachim,** Joakim,
- **Joah,** Yoah, Hebrew, God Is Gracious, Secure
- **Joan,** Joane, Joana, JoAnna,
- **Joannah,** Joey,
- **Jocelyn**, Jocelin,
- **Jodey**, Jodi, Jodie,

- **Joel,** Jole, Hebrew, The Lord Is My God, God's Messenger
- **Joelle**, Joella, French, The Lord Is My God, Beloved
- **Johana**, see Joanna
- **Johann,** Joannes,
- **Johannas**, Johanes,
- **John,** Hebrew, Gift of the Lord, God's Precious Gift
- **Jolan,** Jolanda, Jolanta, Hungarian Violet Flower, Steady Growth
- **Joleane**, Joleen, Joline,
- **Jolene,** Jolayne, Jolean,
- **Jolinn**, Jolynn, English, God Will Increase Reborn,
- **Jonah,** Jona, Jonas,
- **Jonathan**, Johnathan,
- **Jordan,** Jordaan,
- **Joselyn**, Old German, Joyous, Righteous
- **Joseph**, Joe, Joey,
- **Josephina**, Josey, Josie, French
- **Josephine,** Jo, Joey,
- **Josephus,** Jozef, Yosef,
- **Joseseph,** Jose', Jose'e,
- **Joshua**, Jeshua,
- **Julia**, Julee, Juleen, Juli,
- **Julian**, Juliano, Julias,
- **Juliana**, Juliane, Juliann,
- **Julianna**, Julie, Julieann,

- **Julien**, Julio, Jullian, Latin, Youthful, Regenerated
- **Juliene**, Julienne, Julila,
- **Juliet,** Julieta, Juliete,
- **Julietta,** Juliette, Julliet,
- **Julilla,** Julina, Juline,
- **Julisa,** Julissa, Julliana,
- **Julius**, Jule, Jules,
- **Jullianna**, Latin, Youthful, Guided by Faith
- **Jullietta**, French, Youthful, Immovable
- **June,** Junelle, Junia, Latin, Born in the Forth Month, Loving
- **Juri** (see Yuri)
- **Justin**, Justan, Justen,
- **Justina,** Justeen,
- **Justine,** Justinna, French, Upright, Righteous
- **Justinn,** Justinus, Juston,
- **Justinna,** Hebrew, Just, Righteous
- **Justun**, Justyn, Latin, Upright, Righteous

# K

- **Kaarianna**
- **Kadie**, Kady, Kaydee,
- **Kaila,** Kailah, Kailla,
- **Kaila**, Kayla, Middle Eastern, Cherished Adored
- **Kailee**, Kailey, see
- **Kaileen,** Kaylene, Middle Eastern, Sweetheart, Beloved
- **Kaileigh**, Kailey, Kalee,
- **Kaitlin**, Kaetlin,
- **Kaitlinn**, Kaitlyn, Kaitlynn,
- **Kale**, Kayle, Hawaiian, Farmer, Sower of Truth
- **Kalea**, Kahlea, Kahleah,
- **Kaley,** see Kaylee
- **Kali,** Kalli, Hawaiian, Wreath of Flowers, Adorned
- **Kaliana**, see Kaulana
- **Kalianna**, Hawaiian, Famous, Strength of God
- **Kalin**, Kalyn, see Kaylyn
- **Kallan**, Kallen, Kallin,
- **Kanika,** Kanicka,
- **Kannen**, Kanon
- **Kannon,** Kanen,
- **Kanya**, Kania, Kanyah, Thai, Young Lady, Prosperous

- **Kaori,** Kaory, Japanese, Strong, Majestic
- **Kara**, Kaira, Kairah,
- **Karalee**, Karalea,
- **Karalie**, English, Innocent, Righteous
- **Karalynn,** Karilyn,
- **Karen**, Scandinavian, Unblemished, Righteous
- **Karen**, Kaaren, Karan,
- **Karena**, Kareena,
- **Kari**, Karee, Karie, Karri
- **Kariann**, Karianna,
- **Karilynn**, Kariln,
- **Karin**, Kaarin, Kárin,
- **Karina,** Norwegian, Spotless, Purchased
- **Karina,** Karine, Karinna,
- **Karl,** see Carl
- **Karla,** see Carla
- **Karlana**, see Carlana
- **Karlene,** see Carlene
- **Karlin,** Karlee see Carlin
- **Karlina**, see Carlina
- **Karlissa**, see Carlissa
- **Karlynn**, Karlyn, Slavic, Womanly, Valuable
- **Karmen**, see Carmen
- **Karolyn,** Karalyn,
- **Karon,** Karren, Karron,
- **Karriana**,
- **Karrianne,** Keriann,

- **Karriem,** Middle Eastern, Distinguished, Chosen
- **Karylin**, Karylynn,
- **Karyna,** Karynna,
- **Kassandra,**
- **Kassidy**, Cassidy
- **Katareena,** Katerina,
- **Kate,** Cait, Cate, Kait, English, Innocent, Godly Example
- **Kateena,** Katina,
- **Kateland,** Katelin,
- **Katelyn,** Katlyn, Kaytlin,
- **Kathereen,** Katherin,
- **Katherine**, Katharin,
- **Kathleen,** Katheleen,
- **Kathlynn**, Katleen,
- **Kathryn,**
- **Katica,** Katja, Katka,
- **Katie,** Kaytee, Kaytie,
- **Kato,** Katón
- **Katrin,** Katrine, Katrinia,
- **Katrina,** Catarina,
- **Katy**, Catey, Caytee,
- **Katya**, Cata, Catia,
- **Kaylee,** Kaeleah,
- **Kayleen**, Caeleen,
- **Keelan**, Kealyn, Keelen,
- **Keelee**, Keeleigh, Keelie,
- **Keely**, Keilee, Kieley, Gaelic, Beautiful, Trusting

- **Keena,** Kina, Irish, Brave, Given Strength
- **Keenan,** Keanan,
- **Keianna**, Kayana,
- **Keila**, Kaela
- **Keilani**, Keilana,
- **Keira**, Keirra, Kera
- **Keita,** Keeta, Scottish, Enclosed Place, Joyful
- **Keith,** Keath, Scottish, From the Place of Battle, Brave
- **Kelby**, Kelbee, Kelbey,
- **Kelcey,** Kelcie, Kelcy,
- **Keliana**, Kelianna,
- **Kelissa**, English, Fighter, Witness
- **Kellby,** Old German, From the Spring Farm, Petition
- **Kellee,** Kelley, Kelli,
- **Kellia**, Kelliana, Kellie, Irish, Little Friend, Selfless
- **Kellon,** Kellyn see also
- **Kellsea**, Kellsee, Kellsie,
- **Kelly**, Kelia, Keli,
- **Kelsee**, Kelsi, Kelsie,
- **Kelsey**, Kelcea, Kelcee,
- **Kelsy**, Old Norse, From Ship Island, Malleable
- **Kelvin,** Kelvan, Kelvyn, Celtic, From the Narrow River, Reasonable
- **Kemp**, Khemp, English, Champion, Zealous

- **Kenedy,** Kennady, Irish, Ugly-Headed, Obedient
- **Kerry**, Kearie, Keary,
- **Kia,** Kiah, Nigerian, Beginning of the Season, Sign
- **Kiana,** Keanna, Keiana,
- **Kierlyn**, Kierlynn, Kierra,
- **Kiernan**, Kieron, Irish, Little, Blessed
- **Kiesha**, Kisha (see also
- **Kiley**, Kilee, Kileigh, Irish, Attractive, Desirable
- **Killian,** Kilian, Irish, Little Warrior, Attentive
- **Kimber**, Kimberlea,
- **Kimberlee,** Kimberleigh,
- **Kimberley**, Kimberli,
- **Kimberly**, Kim, Kimba,
- **Kinslea**, Kinsleigh,
- **Kinslee**, Old English, Relative, Protected
- **Kira,** Kiri, Kiria, Kirianna,
- **Kirsten**, Keirstan,
- **Kirstine,** Kirston, Kirstyn,
- **Kisa**, Keesa, Keeson,
- **Klaus**, Claas, Claus,
- **Kobi**, Coby
- **Kody**, Cody
- **Koren,** Coren, Corren,
- **Kortney**, see Courtney
- **Krisstal**, Kristal, Kristalee,

- **Kristall,** Kristalyn,
- **Kristeena,** Krysteena,
- **Kristel**, Kristelle, Krystall,
- **Kristen**, Kristan, Kristi,
- **Kristene,** Krystine,
- **Kristian,** Christian
- **Kristie,** Kristii, Kristin,
- **Kristilynn**, Krystalin,
- **Kristina**, Khristina,
- **Kristine**, Kristeen,
- **Kyie,** Bulgarian, Throne, Temple of God
- **Kyla**, Kylah, Kylla, Kyllah
- **Kyle**, Kile, Kylan, Kylan,
- **Kylen,** Kyler, Gaelic, From the Strait Perceptive, Insight
- **Kylen,** Kylyn (see also
- **Kylie,** Kylee, Kyleigh,

# L

- **Lacie,** Lacy, Latin, Joyful, Filled With Praise
- **Lada,** Ladah, Russian, Beauty, Useful
- **Ladonna,** Ladona, La
- **Laela**, Layla
- **Lahela,** Lahaela, Lahaila, Hawaiian, Lamb, Redeemed
- **Laine,** Laina, Lainee,
- **Lainey,** French, Brilliant, Righteous
- **Lamont**, Lamonte,
- **Lana,** Lanna, Lannah, Irish, Attractive, Peaceful
- **Lanae**, Lanai, Lanay,
- **Lance**, Lantz, Launce, German, From the Land, Witness
- **Lancelot,** Launcelot, Old French, Attendant God's Helper
- **Lander,** Landers, Basque Like a Lion, Powerful
- **Lando**, Landro, Portuguese, From the Famous Land, Destined
- **Landon,** Landan, Landin, Old English, From the Grassy Meadow, Comforted
- **Landry**, Landré, French, Ruler, Subject of God

- **Lane**, Laney, Lanie,
- **Lang,** Lange, Old Norse, Tall, Lifted Up
- **Langley,** Langsdon, Old English, From the Long, Meadow Peaceful
- **Langston,** Langsdon, Old English, From the Tall Man's Town, Rescued
- **Lanny,** see Lawrence
- **Larissa**, Larisa, Laryssa, Greek, Cheerful, Grateful
- **Larry**, Laurence, Laurens,
- **Larry**, Lawrence
- **Lars**, Larsen, Larson,
- **Laura**, Latin, Famous God's Gracious, Gift
- **Laurel**, Laural, Laurall,
- **Laurell,** Latin, Laurel, Faithful
- **Lauren**, Lauran,
- **Lauri,** Laurie, Loree,
- **Lauriane**, Laurianna,
- **Laurie,** see Lori
- **Laveda**, Lavedia, Latin, Purified, Blessed
- **Lawrence**, Lanny,
- **Lawton**, Laughton, English, From the Hill Town, Seeker of Truth
- **Layla**, Laela, Laylah,
- **Laylee,** Laylie
- **Leah**, Lea, Léa, Leeah,
- **Leah,** Lia, Liya, American, Meadow, Guided of God
- **Leala**, Lealia, Leial,

- **Leandra**, Leandrea,
- **Leandria**, Leandra, English, Brave as a Lion, Steadfast
- **Leann**, Leann, Leanne,
- **Leanna,** see Liana
- **Leanoer,** Lenora, Lenore,
- **Leia**, (see also Leigh, Lia,
- **Leila**, Laila, Leala, Lelea
- **Lemond**, French, From the Earth, Blessed
- **Lena**, Leena, Lenah,
- **Lennox,** Lenox, Scottish, Placid Stream, God is All-Sufficient
- **Lenny,** Leno, Léonard,
- **Lenore,** Leanore
- **Leo,** Léo, Latin, Lionhearted, Courageous
- **Leon,** Léon, Leone, English, Brave as a Lion, Brave
- **Leona,** Leone, Leonia,
- **Leonard**, Len, Lenard,
- **Leonardo,** Old German, Strong as a Lion, Fearless Spirit
- **Leonorah**, English, Bright Like the Sun, Reflection of Christ
- **Leonore,** Leonora,
- **Leora,** Liora
- **LeRoy**, Old French, Royal, Esteemed
- **Levi**, Leevi, Levey, Levy, Hebrew, Harmonious, Enlightened

- **Levia,** Levya, Hebrew, Attached, One With God
- **Levina,** Leveena, Latin, Flash of Lightning, Ardent Praise
- **Levona,** Livona, Hebrew, Incense, Sacrifice
- **Levya**, Livie, Liviya, Livy,
- **Lewis**, Lew, Lewie, Old English, Safeguard of the People, Righteous
- **Lex,** Lexx, English, Defender of Mankind, Protector
- **Lexey**, Lexee, Lexia,
- **Lexi,** Leksa, Lexa,
- **Leyland**, English, From the Meadowland, Prosperous
- **Lezlee,** Lezley, Lezlie, Scottish, From the Low Meadow, Remembered
- **Lia,** Liah
- **Lian,** Liane, Lianne
- **Liana**, Leana, Leanna,
- **Libbie**, English, Promise of God, Preserved
- **Libby,** Libbee, Libbey,
- **Liberty,** Libertee, Latin, Freedom, Unchained
- **Lida**, Leeda, Lita, Slavic, Love, Beloved
- **Liedon**, Hebrew, Justice is Mine, Defended
- **Liesel,** Leisel, Liesel,

- **Liezel,** Liezl, Lisel, German, Oath of God, Promise
- **Lila**, Hebrew, Dark Beauty, Bringer of Light
- **Liliana,** Liliane, Liljana,
- **Lilith,** Lillith, Hebrew, Night Owl, Wise
- **Lillian,** Lilli, Lilia, Lilian,
- **Lilliana,** Lillianna,
- **Lillyann,** Lily, Latin, Purity, Shining Light
- **Lin,** Linh, Linn
- **Lina**, Greek, Gentle, Blessed Peacemaker
- **Lincoln**, Lincon, Old English, From the Pool Town, Victorious
- **Linda**, Linnea, Linnie,
- **Lindee**, Lindey, Lindi,
- **Lindel,** Lyndel, Lyndell, Anglo-Saxon,
- **Lindie,** Lindy, American, Lovely, Witness
- **Lindon,** Lynden, English, From the Lime Tree Hill, Excellent Worth
- **Lindsee,** Lindsi, Lindsie,
- **Lindsey**, Lindsay,
- **Lindsy**, Lindzee, Linsay,
- **Linsey**, Linsi, Linsie,
- **Linus,** Linas, Greek, Fair-Haired, Treasurer of Wisdom and Knowledge
- **Linzey**, Lynnzey, Lynsay,

- **Liona,** Latin, Lioness, Courageous Spirit
- **Lionel,** Lional, Lionell,
- **Liora**, Leora, Hebrew, Glowing Light, Brilliance
- **Lisa,** Leesa, Liesa, Liisa,
- **Lisanne,** Lise
- **Lisette**, Lissette, French, Promise of God, One With Christ
- **Lloyd**, Loyd, Welsh, Wise, Seeker of Holiness
- **Locke**, Lock, Old English, From the Forest, Wise
- **Logan,** Logen, Celtic, From the Little Hollow, Devoted to God
- **Lois**, Greek, Desired, Established in Truth
- **Lola**, Lolita, Latin, Owned With Compassion and Grace, Perceptive Insight
- **Loman,** Lomán, Serbian, Delicate, Loving
- **London**, Londan,
- **Lonie**, German, Lioness, Courageous
- **Lonna,** Lona, Loni,
- **Lonnie,** Lon, Lonn,
- **Lonny**, English, Ready for Battle, God's Soldier
- **Lora,** Laura
- **Loren,** Larian, Larien,
- **Lorence**, Lorentz,

- **Lori,** Latin, Crowned With Honor, Victorious
- **Lorrie**, (see also Laura), English, Crowned With Honor, Hopeful
- **Louis,** Lou, Louie, Luigi,
- **Louise**, Louisa, Luisa,
- **Lowell,** Lovell, Lowel, Latin, Little Wolf, Peaceful
- **Luann**, Luana, Luanna,
- **Luanne**, Hebrew, Graceful Warrior, Righteous
- **Luciann,** Lucie, Lucienne,
- **Ludwig**, Ludvig, German, Famous Warrior, Gifted
- **Luis**, Old German, Famous Warrior, Declarer of God
- **Lydia**, Lidi, Lidia, Lidiya, Greek, Womanly, Beautiful Light
- **Lyle**, Lisle, Lysle, Old French, From the Island, Joyous Spirit
- **Lynda,** Spanish, Beautiful, Excellent Virtue
- **Lyndon**, Lindan, Linden,
- **Lynell,** Lynell, Lynnelle, English, Pretty Virtuous
- **Lynelle,** Linell, Linnell,
- **Lynsee,** Lynsey, Lynzey,

# M

- **Maayan,** Maayana,
- **Macdonald,** McDonald,
- **Maci,** Macie, French, From the Matthew's Estate, Enlightened
- **Macia,** Macya, Polish, Wished-for, Blameless
- **Macy,** Macee, Macey,
- **Madalaina**, Madaline,
- **Madisson**, Old English, Child of the Valiant Warrior, Brave
- **Madlen,** Madlin,
- **Madoline**, Greek, Magnificent, Prayerful
- **Madonna**, Madona, Latin, My Lady, Pure
- **Magdalina,** Magdaline,
- **Magdalyn**, Magdelana,
- **Magdelena**, Magdelene,
- **Magdelina,** Magdeline,
- **Maggie**, Maggee, Maggi, Greek, Pearl Of Great, Value
- **Magnus,** Magnes, Latin, Great, Privileged
- **Malcolm**, Malcom, Scottish, Diligent Servant, Teachable Spirit
- **Malerie,** Mallerie,
- **Mali**, Malee, Maley, Malí
- **Malia,** Maleah, Maleia,

- **Malin**, Mallin, Mallon,
- **Mallory**, Mallari, Mallary,
- **Malorie,** Malory, German, Counselor, Joyful
- **Manleigh**, Irish, Heroic, Victorious Spirit
- **Manley,** Manlea,
- **Manning**, Maning, English, Child of the Her,o Obedient
- **Mannuel**, Manny
- **Manon,** Mannon, French, Wished-for, Fulfilled
- **Manuel,** Manni,
- **Marcellus,** Marsel,
- **Marcia,** Marcee, Marci,
- **Margeret**, Margerite,
- **Maria,** Marea, Mareah,
- **Marian,** Mariana,
- **Mariane,** Mariann,
- **Marianna,** Marianne,
- **Marie,** Maree (see also
- **Mariel,** Marial, Mariela,
- **Mariele**, Mariella,
- **Marika,** Marica, Marrika,
- **Marilu**, Marilow, Marylou, American, Bitter Grace, Blessed
- **Marilynn,** Marralin,
- **Marina,** Marena,
- **Marino**, Latin, Warlike, Powerful
- **Mario,** Marios, Marrio, Italian, Sailor, Regenerated

- **Marion,** Marian
- **Maris,** Marisa, Marise,
- **Mark,** Marc, Marciano,
- **Marlon,** Marlin, Welsh, From the Hill by the Sea, Victorious Spirit
- **Marly,** Marlys, Marlysa,
- **Marrissia**, Marysa,
- **Marsden,** Marsdon, English, From the Boundary Valley, Preserved
- **Marsello**, Latin, Industrious Worker, Strong in Spirit
- **Marsha**, Marsi, Marsi,
- **Marthina,** Martinia,
- **Martie,** Martika, Marty,
- **Martin,** Martan, Marten,
- **Martina,** Martel, Martelle,
- **Martinez**, Marton, Marty,
- **Martiza,** Martoya,
- **Martrina,** Martyna, Hispanic, Lady of the House, Virtuous
- **Marylin,** English, Bitterness, Sacrifice of Praise
- **Marylou,** Marilu
- **Maryssa,** Meris, Merisa,
- **Mathew**, Mathias,
- **Mathilda**, Tilda, Tillie, German, Noble Lady, Beloved
- **Matthew,** Mateo,
- **Mauriell,** Maurielle
- **Mavis,** Mayvis, French, Songbird, Praise

- **Maximillian**, Max, Maxx, Latin, Greatest in Excellence, Teachable Spirit
- **Maxwell**, Max, Maxx, Scottish, From the Great Spring, Righteous
- **May,** Mae, Maye, Hebrew, Gift of God, Blessed
- **Maya**, Mayah
- **Maylin,** Old English, Little Warrior, Champion
- **Maynard**, Ménard, Old English, Powerful, Spirit of Praise
- **Mayo,** Maiyo, Irish, From the Yew-Tree, Plain Heart of Praise
- **McArthur**, Scottish, Child of the Brave, Forgiven
- **McGwire,** Irish, Child of the Fair One, Trustworthy
- **McKenzee**, McKenzie, Gaelic, Child of the Wise Leader, Witness
- **McKinnley,** Irish, Child of the Scholarly Ruler, Peaceful
- **Meagann,** Meagen,
- **Medina,** Medaena,
- **Medora,** Medorra, English, Mother's Gift, Blessing
- **Meg,** Megan, Megen,
- **Megan,** Maegan,
- **Meggie**, Meghan,
- **Melani**, Mélanie,
- **Melanie,** Melanie,

- **Melissa**, Malissa,
- **Mélissa,** Mellisa,
- **Mellicent,** Millee, Millie,
- **Melvin**, Malvin, Mel, Middle English, Reliable Friend, Excellent Virtue
- **Mendel**, Mendell, Hebrew, Wisdom, Studious
- **Menora,** Manora, Hebrew, Candelabrum, Witness
- **Mercedes,** Mersade, Latin, Gift, Esteemed
- **Merissa**, English, Bitterness, Eternally Steadfast
- **Merlin,** Merle, Merlen, Old English, Falcon, Courageous
- **Merrall,** Merryl, Meryll
- **Mervin,** Marvin
- **Meryl,** Meral, Merel,
- **Mia,** Meah, Miah
- **Michael,** Mekhail,
- **Michaele,** Michaelle,
- **Michah,** Mycah, Hebrew, Who Is Like God? Reverent
- **Michal**, Machelle,
- **Michala,** Michayle,
- **Mickey**, Mickie, Micky,
- **Mikaela**, Mikalya, Mikyla,
- **Mike**, Mikhael, Mikhail,
- **Miki,** Mikki, Mychal,
- **Milan**, Milen, Mylan,
- **Milian**
- **Milana**, Milanna, Milania

- **Milana**, Milena, Hebrew, Tower, Secure
- **Mildred,** Midge, Mildrid, Old English, Gentle Spirit, Loving Spirit
- **Millissa,** Missi, Missie,
- **Milly,** Old German, Industrious, Strong Spirit
- **Milo**, Mylo, Old German, Generous, Helpful Spirit
- **Milton**, Milt, Mylton, English From the Mill Town Blessed of God
- **Mimi,** Mimee, Mimie,
- **Mimie,** Mimii, English, Wished-for, Spiritual Passion
- **Mina,** Mini, Minni,
- **Mindie**, Myndee, Myndie, English, Sweet as Honey, Genuine
- **Mindy,** Mindee, Mindi,
- **Mingan**, Mingen, Native American, Gray Wolf, Vigilant
- **Minnie,** Minny, Old German, Love, Cherished
- **Miron**, Greek, Fragrant Ointment, Peaceful Praise
- **Miron,** Miran
- **Mischel,** Mishayle,
- **Misha,** Mischa, Mishka, Russian, Who Is Like God? Disciple
- **Molli**, Mollie, English, Desired, Righteous
- **Molly**, Mollee, Molley,

- **Mona,** Monna, Moyna, Irish, Noble, Reflection of Wisdom
- **Monica**, Moneka, Moni,
- **Morris**, Maurice
- **Murphy,** Murfey, Irish, Sea Warrior, Full of Praise
- **Murray**, Murrey, Gaelic, Sailor, Discerning
- **Mustafa,** Mostafa,
- **Myla**, Mylah, Mylea,
- **Mylen,** Mylon Italian From Milan Witness

# N

- **Nadia,** Latin, Nest, Spiritual Potenial
- **Nadine**, Nadean,
- **Nancy**, Nan, Nana,
- **Napoleon,** Greek, Lion of the Woodland, Bold
- **Natalie**, Natalea,
- **Natasha**, natachia,
- **Nealon,** Neile, Neill,
- **Neil**, Neal, Neale,
- **Neilon**, Irish, Champion, Beloved
- **Nellee,** Nelley, Nelli, English, Shining, Witness
- **Nellie,** Nel, Nell, Nelle,
- **Nelson**, Neilson, Nelsen,
- **Neriah,** Neri, Neria,
- **Nerissa,** Narissa, English, Sea Nymph, Expectant
- **Neva,** Neyva, English, New, Obedient
- **Nevan**, Neven, Nevin,
- **Nevill,** Old French, From the New Town, Compassionate Spirit
- **Neville**, Nevil, Nevile,
- **Nevon**, Navin, Irish, Holy, Righteous
- **Newell**, Newall, Middle English, From the New Hall, Sincere

- **Newton,** Newtyn, Middle English, From the New Town, Helpful Counselor
- **Nichalas**, Nicholas,
- **Nigel,** Niegel, Nigell,
- **Nikolai,** Nikolas,
- **Nikolaus,** Nikolai, Nikoli,
- **Nikolette**, Nikolle,
- **Nikolos**, Nycholas,
- **Nikolyn**, Niquole, Nykola,
- **Nils**, Niels, Niles, Scandinavian, Champion, Triumphant
- **Ninah**, English, Grace of God, Delivered
- **Nixon**, English, Son of the Victor, Overcomer
- **Noel,** Noél, Noël, Noela,
- **Noele,** Noelia, Noelle,
- **Noella,** Noelle, Latin, Christmas Child, Precious Gift
- **Nola**, Nuala Latin Small Bell Harmonious
- **Norma,** Noma, Latin, Perfection, Model of Excellence
- **Norman,** Norm,
- **Normand**, Normen,
- **Normie**, Old English, Man From the North, Courageous Spirit
- **Norris,** Noris, Old English, Northerner, Wise
- **Norton,** Nortan, Middle English, From the North Town, Integrity

- **Nydia,** Slavic, Hopeful, Blessed
- **Nykolas**, Nikita, Greek, Victory of the People, Triumphant Spirit

# O

- **Oakley,** Oaklee,
- **Octavio**, Octavien,
- **Octavious**, Latin, Eighth, Abiding in God
- **Octavius**, Octavian,
- **Odell,** Odie, Middle English, From the Wooded Hill, Hopeful
- **Odella,** Odeleya, Hebrew, I Will Praise God, Thankful Spirit
- **Odessa**, Odyssa, Greek, Long Voyage, Preserved
- **Odysseua**, Odesseus, Greek, Wrathful, Righteous
- **Olga,** Olya, Scandinavian, Holy, Wise
- **Oliver**, Olley, Ollie,
- **Olivia**, Olive, Olivea,
- **Oprah**, Hebrew, Runaway
- **Orin,** Hebrew, Ash Tree, Blessed
- **Orion**, Orien, Greek, Son of Fire, Zealous
- **Orlando,** Orlanda,
- **Orli,** Ori, Orlie, Hebrew, My Light, Fearless
- **Orlondo**, Italian, Famous Throughout the Land, Renowned
- **Orpah,** Ophra, Opra,

- **Oscar,** Oskar, Old English, Divine Spearman, Appointed of God
- **Osmond,** Osmund, Old English, Divine Protector, God's Warrior
- **Oswald**, Osvaldo,
- **Otis**, Ottis, Greek, Keen of Hearing, Open to Divine Inspiration
- **Otto,** Oto, German, Prosperous, Esteemed
- **Owen,** Owens, Greek, Distinguished, Pleasant to Look Upon
- **Oxford,** Oxforde, Old English, The Place Where the Oxen Cross the Restful
- **Oya,** Oiya Miwok Called Forth Witness
- **Ozzie**, Hebrew, Courage, Overcomer

# P

- **Pablo,** Paublo, Spanish, Small Bell, Great Faith
- **Palmer**, Palmar, Old English, Peaceful, Pilgrim Bringer of Peace
- **Pamela,** Pam, Pamala,
- **Paris**, Parras, Parris, Greek, Attractive, Godly
- **Park**, Parke, Chinese, Cyprus Tree, Blessed
- **Parker,** Parkker, Middle English, Guardian of the Park, Spiritual Light
- **Parnell,** Parnel, Pernell, French, Little Peter, Faithfulness
- **Patience,** Paishence, English, Endurance, Fortunate, Firmness of Spirit
- **Paul,** Pasha, Pauley,
- **Paula,** Paula, Paolina,
- **Paulette**, Paulina,
- **Pauli,** Paulis, Paolo,
- **Pauline,** Paulla, Latin, Small Loving
- **Paulo**, Paulus, Pavel, Latin, Small, Dynamo of Energy and Faith
- **Paxton,** Paxon, Paxten, Old English, From the Peaceful Town, Prepared
- **Payne**, Paine, Latin, From the Country, Sacred

- Peggy, Peg, Pegg, Peggi English Pearl Promise
- **Peirce**, English, Stone, Strong in Spirit
- **Pele**, Pelé, Peleh, Hebrew, Miracle, Strong Faith
- **Peli**, Pelí, Basque, Happy, Filled With Joy
- **Penelope**, Pennelope,
- **Perry**, Parry
- **Pervis**, Purvis, Latin, Passage, Messenger
- **Pete**, Péter, Petr, Petey,
- **Peter**, Peder, Petar,
- **Petra**, Petrina, Pietra, Greek, Small Rock, Strong and Everlasting
- **Peyton,** Paiton, Payden,
- **Phebe,** Phoebe, Greek, Bright, Cherished
- **Philipp**, Philippe, Phill,
- **Phoebe**, see Phebe
- **Phylicia**, see Felecia
- **Phyllis,** Phylliss, Greek, Green Branch, Youthful Trust
- **Pia,** Piya, Italian, Devoted, Focused
- **Pierce**, Pearce, Peerce,
- **Pilar,** Pillar, Latin, Pillar, Strong in Faith
- **Piper,** English, Pipe Player, Joyous Spirit

- **Piran,** Pieran, Irish, Prayer, Supplicant
- **Porter**, Port, Latin, Gatekeeper, Watchful Spirit
- **Presley,** Presleigh, Old English, From the Priest's Meadow, Peaceful Spirit
- **Preston**, Prestan, Old English, From the Priest's Home, Consecrated to God
- **Price**, Pryce, Welsh, Son of the Ardent One, Eager
- **Pricilla,** Priscila, Prisilla,

# Q

- **Quenby**, Quenbie, Swedish, Feminine, Holy

- **Quimby**, Quinby, Scandinavian, From the Queen's Estate, Vigilant Spirit

- **Quincy**, Quincey, Quinci,

- **Quinn**, Quin, Gaelic, Intelligent, Godly Insight

- **Quintana,** Quinta,

- **Quinton**, Quintus,

# R

- **Raanan**, Ranaan, Ranan
- **Rachaele**, Rachal,
- **Rachel**, Rachael,
- **Rachele**, Racquel,
- **Rachelle,** Rochelle
- **Radleigh**, English, From the Reed Meadow, Spirit-Filled
- **Raechel**, Raechele,
- **Raechell**, Raeschelle,
- **Raelene**, Raeleen,
- **Raelina,** Raelle, Raelyn,
- **Raelynn,** Rayele,
- **Raina,** Raenah, Rainna
- **Rainor,** Rainar, Rainer,
- **Ralph,** Ralf
- **Ramón**, Ramone (see
- **Randi,** Randalin,
- **Randie,** Randie, Randii, English, Shield, Guarded
- **Randoph,** Randolf, Old English, Shield, Established in Peace
- **Randy,** Ranndy, English, Shield, Protected
- **Ranee**, Rania
- **Ranger,** Rainger, Range, French, Keeper of the Forest, Covenant
- **Ranie**, Hebrew, My Song, Praise

- **Ranios**, Old German, Mighty Army, Strength of God
- **Ranon**, Ranen, Rani,
- **Raphael,** Raphaela
- **Rea**, Reah, Reha (see
- **Reagan**, Reaganne,
- **Reba,** Reva, Rheba, English, Bound, Witness
- **Rebeca**, Rébecca,
- **Rebecca**, Rabecca,
- **Reena**, Rena
- **Reesa**, Resa, Reesha,
- **Reese**, Reece, Rhys, Welsh, Enthusiastic, Dedicated
- **Reeve**, Reaves, Reeves, Middle English, Steward, Servant
- **Regan**, Raegan,
- **Reggie**, Regi, Regie,
- **Regina**, Regeena, Reggi,
- **Reginald**, Reg, Reggie,
- **Reginia**, Reginna, Latin, Queen, Gracious
- **Regis**, Reggis, Latin, Regal, Honored
- **Reid,** Raed, Reade,
- **Reiko**, Reyko, Japanese, Sign, Miraculous
- **Remi,** Remee, Rémi,
- **René**, Raeneé, Rainato,
- **Renée,** French, Born Again, Joyful
- **Reubin**, Rheuben,

- **Rex**, Rexx, Latin, King, Leadership
- **Reyanna,** Reyanne,
- **Reynald**, Reynaldo,
- **Rhea**, Rhaya, Rhéa,
- **Rhiauna**, Rhyan,
- **Rhoda,** Rhodi, Rhody, Greek, From the Island of Roses, God's Unfolded Love
- **Rhodes,** Rhoads, Greek, From the Island of Roses, Formed of God
- **Richard**, Ric, Ricardo,
- **Richards**, Richie, Rick,
- **Richele**, Richella (see
- **Richelle**, Richela,
- **Richmond,** Richmon, French, From the Hill of Wealthy, Vegetati Nourished
- **Rickey**, Ricki, Rickie,
- **Ricky**, Rico, Ricqui,
- **Ricquie**, Rik, Riki, Rikk,
- **Roanna,** Indo-Pakistani, Stringed Instrument, Joyful Praise
- **Robert**, Bob, Bobb,
- **Roberta**, Birdee, Birdie,
- **Roberto**, Roberts,
- **Robertson**, Robinson,
- **Robin,** Robbin, Robbyn,
- **Robyn,** Robynn, English, Shining Fame, Victorious Spirit
- **Rodnee**, Anglo-Saxon, From the Clearing on the Island, Joyful
- **Rodney**, Rod, Rhodney,

- **Rodrigo**, Rodriguez,
- **Rodrik**, Rodrique,
- **Rogan**, Rogann, Irish, Redhead, Persevering
- **Roger**, Rodger, Rog,
- **Rolland**, Rollando, Rolle,
- **Rollie**, Rowland, Old German, Famous Throughout the Land, Full of Wisdom
- **Ronia,** Ronnee, Ronney,
- **Ronni**, Ronee, Roni,
- **Ronnie,** Ronny, Ronya English, Power, Strength
- **Rosalin**, Rosalina,
- **Rosalinda**, Rosalyn,
- **Rosalynn**, Roselynn,
- **Rosamond,** Rosamund Old German Guardian Protector of Truth
- **Rosannah**, Rosangela,
- **Rose Anne,**
- **Rose**, Rosa, Rosey,
- **Roseann**, Rose Ann,
- **Roseanna**, Rosana,
- **Roseannah**, Rossana,
- **Rosi,** Rosie, Rosy, Roza,
- **Rosine,** Rosina, Italian, Cherished, Bold
- **Ross**, Roess, Gaelic, Knight, Victorious
- **Rossanna,** Rozana,

- **Rowen**, Rowan, Irish, Red, Purchased
- **Rowena**, Rowina, Welsh, Peaceful, Wise
- **Roxane,** Roxann, Roxi,
- **Roxanne**, Roxana,
- **Roxie**, Roxy, Persian, Sunrise, Heavenly
- **Roy**, Roi, French, King, Seeker of Wisdom
- **Royce**, Roice, Old English, Son of the King, Tranquil Spirit
- **Roza**, Rozee, Rozy, Latin, Rose, God's Gracious Gift
- **Rozália,** Rozalee,
- **Rozalie**, Rozalin,
- **Rozalyn**, Rozalyn,
- **Ruben**, Rubin, Hebrew, Behold, A Son Wondrous Recognition
- **Rubi**, Rubie, French, Beautiful Jewel, Full of Grace
- **Ruby**, Rubia, Rubey,
- **Rudolph,** Rudi, Rudy, Old German, Great and Famous, Resourceful
- **Rufus,** Ruffus, Latin, Red-Haired, Excellent Virtue
- **Rune,** Roone, Swedish, Secret, Guarded of God
- **Russell,** Russ, Russel,
- **Rylee**, Rylie, Irish, Valiant, Protected

# S

- **Sabina**, Sabinna,

- **Sabrina,** Sabreena,

- **Sadee**, Saydee, English, Princess, Beautiful

- **Sadhana**, Indo-Pakistani, Devotion, Persistent

- **Sadie,** S'ade, Sad'e,

- **Safron**, Saffrón, English, Flower, Valuable Spice

- **Sage,** Saige, English, Wise, Discerning

- **Sahara,** Saharah, English, Wilderness, Strengthened

- **Sahra**, Sahra, Sara,

- **Salina,** Salena, Saleena

- **Salli**, Sallie, Old English, Princess, Beloved

- **Sally,** Sallee, Salley,

- **Salvador**, Sal,

- **Sammie**, Sammuel,

- **Sammy**, Samuele, Hebrew, God Has Heard, Instructed of God

- **Samuel**, Sam, Samm,

- **Sandee**, Sandi, Sandie,

- **Sanders**, Sander,

- **Sandra,** Sahndra,

- **Sandrea,** Sandreea,

- **Sandreia**, Sandira,

- **Sandy,** Saundra, Sondra,

- **Santiago**, Sántiago Spanish Saint Gifted

- **Sanya,** Sania, Saniya, Indo-Pakistani, Born on Saturday, Believer

- **Sapphira**, Safire, Saffire,

- **Sapphire**, Greek, Gem, Precious

- **Sarah**, Saara, Saarah,

- **Savana,** Savannah,

- **Savanna,** Savauna,

- **Sawyer,** Soiyer, English, Wood Worker, Gifted

- **Saxon,** Sax, Saxen, Middle English, Swordsman, Valorous

- **Scott**, Scot, Scottie,

- **Scotty**, Old English, From Scotland, Temple of God

- **Sean**, Séan, Seán,

- **Sebastian**, Sabastien,

- **Sébastien**, Greek, Venerable, Esteemed

- **Sebina,** Sebinah, Latin, Planter of Vines, Spiritual Discernment

- **Seeley**, see Ceeley

- **Selaam**, Ethiopian, Peaceful, Content

- **Selam,** Saalam, Salaam,

- **Selby**, Selbey, English, From the Mansion, Child of God

- **Selena,** Selenia, Selina,

- **Selma**, Selmah, Zelma, Celtic, Divinely Protected, Enlightened Spirit

- **Selyna**, Sylena, Sylina,

- **Serena,** Sarina, Sereena,

- **Serenah**, Serrenna,

- **Shaina**, Shaena,

- **Shana,** Shanae,

- **Shanna,** Shannah,

- **Sharai**, Sharaiah,

- **Shauna**

- **Shawne**, Shawnn,

- **Sheila**, Sheela, Sheelah, Beginning Miraculous

- **Shelbey**, Shelbie, Shellby, Old English, From the Estate on the Slope, Faithful Steward

- **Shelby,** Shelbee,

- **Sheldon,** Shelden,

- **Sheliah,** Shiela, Shyla, English, Blind, Wise

- **Silas**, Sylas, Latin, From the Forest, Steadfast in Trust

- **Silvanna,** Silvia, Silvania,

- **Silvia**, Sylvia

- **Simba,** Symba Swahili Lion Blessed

- **Simon**, Shimon,

- **Simone**, Samona,

- **Siona**, Siauna, Siaunna,

- **Sionna,** Hebrew, Apex, Productive

- **Skelly,** Skelley, Gaelic, Storyteller, Treasure of Knowledge

- **Skye**, Sky, Middle Eastern, Supplier of Water, Miraculous Creation

- **Skyelar**, Skyla, Skylah,

- **Skylar**, Skylee, Sklie,

- **Skyler**, Schylar, Schyler,

- **Skyllar**, Skyller, Skylor, Dutch, Scholar, Wise

- **Sophia**, Sofi, Soffi,

- **Stacey,** Stacia, Stacee,

- **Stacie,** Stacy, Stasia,

- **Stafanie**, Staffany,

- **Sullivan**, Sulley, Sullie,

- **Summer**, English, Summer, Ordained

- **Summer**, Sommer

- **Susanna**, Susanne, Sue,

- **Suzann**, Suzanna,

- **Suzanne,** Suzette, Suzi,

- **Suzie,** Suzy, Hebrew, Graceful, Lily Purity

- **Sven**, Svein, Swen, Scandinavian, Youth Loving

- **Sydnee,** Sydney, Sydnie,

- **Sydney**, Sidney

- **Sylvana**, Sylvanya,

- **Sylvester**, Silvester,

- **Sylvia,** Silva, Silvana,

# T

- **Tal,** Talley, Tally, Hebrew, Rain, Blessing

- **Tala**, Tallah, Native American, Stalking Wolf, Tamed

- **Talbot**, Talbott, Old German, Bright Valley, Promise

- **Talia**, Talaya, Talea,

- **Tani,** Tahnee, Tahnie,

- **Tania**, Tahnia, Tahniya,

- **Tanna**, Tannia, Tannis,

- **Tarah**, Taira, Tairra,

- **Taria,** Tarin, Taris,

- **Tasmine**, Tasmin, English, Twin, Worthy

- **Tereese**, Terese, Teresa,

- **Terry** (see also Tarrant), Latin, Tender, Gently Formed

- **Terry**, Therese, Thérèse,

- **Thelma**, Thellma, Greek, Willful, Strong in Spirit

- **Theodore**, Ted, Teddie,

- **Theresa**, Taresa, Tarisa,

- **Theressa**, Thereza,

- **Theron**, Theran, Therron, Greek, Hunter, Efficient

- **Thomas,** Thom,

- **Thompson**, Tom, Tomás,

- **Thor**, Thorin, Old Norse, Thunder, God's Warrior

- **Tia,** Téa, Teeya, Teia,

- **Tiana,** Teana, Teanna,

- **Tiandra**, Tianika, Tilia, Spanish, Aunt, Pure

- **Tianna**, Greek, Princess, Praised

- **Tiara**, Tearra, Teira,

- **Tiarra,** Tiárra, Tiera,

- **Tierney**, Tiernan, Irish, Lordly, Gracious Spirit

- **Tifaney**, Tifani, Tifanie,

- **Tiffiny,** Tiffney, Tifnee,

- **Tifnie**, Tifny, Tiphanee,

- **Tilden**, Tildan, Old English, From the Blessed Valley, Peaceful Spirit

- **Tiltan,** Tilton, Hebrew, Clover, Blossom

- **Timmothy**, Timmy,

- **Timothé**, Timothée,

- **Timothi,** Tymothee,

- **Timothy**, Tim, Timmie,

- **Tina,** Teena, Téna, Tyna, English, Anointed, Protected

- **Tino,** Tíno, Hispanic, Venerable, Promised Hope

- **Tobiah**, Tobie, Tobi,

- **Tobias**, Tobee, Tobey,

- **Toby**, Hebrew, The Lord Is Good, God's Workmanship

- **Tracey**, Trace, Tracee,

- **Traci**, Tracia, Tracie,

- **Traciya,** Tracy, Tracya,

- **Traecee,** Traecey,

- **Traicey**, Trasee, Trasey

- **Trent**, Trente, English, Rapid Stream, Renewed

- **Trenten,** Trentin, Old English,

- **Trenton,** Trendon,

- **Trever**, Irish, Prudent, Righteous

- **Trevor**, Trev, Trevar,

- **Trey,** Trae, Trai, Middle English, Third, Sacrifice

- **Treysa**, Treyssa, Greek, Harvester, Bountiful Spirit

- **Tria**, Triana, Trianna,

- **Trilbie**, English Hat Covered

- **Trilby**, Trilbee, Trilbey,

- **Trina**, Treena, Treina,

- **Trinette,** Trinice,

- **Tristen**, Trista, Tristan,

- **Tristia**, Tristian, Tristiana,

- **Trixie,** Trix, Trixi, American, Bringer of Joy, Peaceful

- **Troy**, Troi, Troye, Gaelic, Foot Soldier, Steadfast

- **Truman**, Trumann English Honest Faithful

- **Trusten,** Trustan, Trustin

- **Tucker**, Old English, Folder of Cloth, Efficient

- **Tullis,** Tullias, Tullius, Latin, Rank, Admirable

- **Tyfanny**, Tyfanni, Tyffini,

- **Tyler,** Ty, Tylar, Tyller,

- **Tylor**, Middle English, Tile Maker, Resourceful

- **Tymothy**, Greek, Honor to God, Blessed of God

- **Typhanee**, Typhany, English, Divine Showing, Beloved

- **Tyra**, Tyraa, Tyrah,

- **Tyshia,** (see also Taesha), English, Joy, Thankful

- **Tyson**, Tison, Tyce,

# U

- **Ulani,** Ulana, Ulanna,
- **Ulric,** Ulrik, Old German, Ruler of All, Regenerated
- **Ulrica,** Ulrika, Old German, Ruler, Strong in Virtue
- **Ulysses**, Ulisses, Latin, One Who Detests, Seeker of Truth
- **Urban**, Urbain, Latin, From the City, Peaceful
- **Urbana,** Urbanna, Latin, From the City, Majestic
- **Uri,** Uree, Urii
- **Uriah**, Urias, Uriyah, Hebrew, God Is Light, Excellent Virtue
- **Uriel,** Uriela, Urieli,

# V

- **Vera,** Vara, Vira, Latin, Truth, Strong in Virtue
- **Viktoria**, Viktoriana,
- **Venus,** Veenus, Latin, Love, Greatest Power
- **Vianna,** Viana
- **Vance,** Vanse, English, Thresher, Hard Worker
- **Vivian**, Viv, Vivia,
- **Vincent**, Vincente,
- **Valery,** Vallerie, Valllery,
- **Vandie,** Vandda
- **Verina**, Verity
- **Viktory,** Viktorya, Latin, Conqueror, Triumphant Spirit
- **Vlade,** Vladé, Russian, Famous Prince, Upright
- **Vallory**, Latin, Strength, Spiritual Purpose
- **Veronica**, Varonica,
- **Valin**, Vaylin
- **Vivana,** Vivianne,
- **Vanda,** Vandelia, Vandi,
- **Victoria,** Vicci, Vickee,
- **Vallie,** Vally, Latin, Strong, God's Leader
- **Varina,** Vareena,

- **Vanessa,** Vanesa,
- **Vanissa**, Venessa, Greek, Butterfly, Free Spirit
- **Violet,** Vi, Viola, Violette,
- **Van,** Vann, Dutch, Water Dam, Forgiving
- **Virginia**, Virg, Virgenia, Latin, Pure, Unblemished
- **Viktor**, Latin, Conqueror, Triumphant Spirit
- **Vicki,** Vickie, Vicky,
- **Valerie,** Val, Valarae,
- **Veronika,** Véronique,
- **Victor**, Vic, Victer, Vik,
- **Vivien**, Vivienne Latin Lively Joyous Spirit
- **Valerie**, Valeree, Valeri,

# W

- **Wade**, Wayde, Old English, One Who Advances, Generous Spirit
- **Wagner**, Waggner, Old German, Wagon Maker, Trusting Spirit
- **Walker**, Wallker, English, Cloth Cleaner, Diligent
- **Wallace,** Wallach,
- **Wallis**, Wally, Walsh,
- **Walter,** Walt Old, German, Powerful Ruler, Strong Protector
- **Walton,** Walt, English, From the Fortified Town, Freedom of Spirit
- **Warner**,
- **Welby,** Wellby, Old English, From the Near Well, Trusting Spirit
- **Weldon,** Welden Old English From Hill Near the Well Preserved
- **Wendee**, Wendey,
- **Wendell**, Wendal,
- **Wendi,** Wendie
- **Wendy,** Wenda,
- **Wesley,** Wes, Weslee,
- **Westlee**, Westley, English, From the Western, Meadow Steadfast
- **Whitley**, Whitlee,
- **Whitnée**, Whitneigh,
- **Whitney,** Whitnee,

- **Whitnie**, Whittany,
- **Whittney,** Witney,
- **Wiley**, Will, Wiley, Willie,
- **Wilhelm,** Willhelm, Old German, Determined Guardian, Wise
- **William**, Bill, Billy, Wil,
- **Willis**, Willus, English, Son of the Guardian, Cautious
- **Willow**, Wilow, English, Willow Tree, Great Hope
- **Willy,** Wilson, Old German, Resolute Protector, Noble Spirit
- **Wyatt**, Wyat, Wyatte, Old French, Little Warrior, Immoveable
- **Wyman**, Wymon, Old English, Warrior, Determined
- **Wynn,** Wyn, Wynette,
- **Wynne**, Welsh, Fair, Righteous
- **Wynnona,** Wynona, Sioux, First-Born Daughter, Peaceful
- **Wynston**, Old English, From the Friendly Town, Trusting

# *X*

- **Xandriana**, Xandria
- **Xenia,** Xena
- **Xylina,** Greek, Wood, One of Integrity
- **Xavier**, Xavian, Xavion,
- **Xandra**, Xandraea,
- **Xuan,** Xuann, Vietnamese, Spring, Refreshed
- **Xuxa**, Xùxa, Brazilian, Lily, Beautiful
- **Xaven,** Xavon, Zavier,
- **Xylia**, Xyleah, Xyliana,

# *Y*

- **Yarianna**, Yaryna, Russian, Peace, Secure
- **Yelina**, Yelana, Yelanna
- **Yasmine**, Yasmen,
- **Yago**, see Iago
- **Yul,** Yule, Yuul, Mongolian, Beyond the Horizon, Worshiper
- **Yadin**, Yadeen, Yadín, Hebrew, God Will Judge, Righteous
- **Yvonne**, Ivette, Ivonne,
- **Yannam,** Yannah,
- **Yannika**, (see also Jana), Polish, Gift of God, Purchased
- **Yves,** Ives, French, Little Archer, Trusting Spirit

# Z

- **Zuri**, Zuria, Zuriya, Swahili, Beautiful, Messenger
- **Zacccary**, Zach,
- **Zia**, Zea, Zeah, Zeya, Middle Eastern, Light Fearless
- **Zerlina**, Zerleyna, Spanish, Dawn, Blessed
- **Zabrina**, Sabrina
- **Zena,** Zeena, Zeenia,
- **Zaynah**, Zayna
- **Zoe**, Zoa, Zöe, Zoé,
- **Zephaniah,** Zephan,
- **Zackarie**, Zackary,
- **Zephyr**, Zephria,
- **Zeenya**, Zeina
- **Zorina**, Zori, Zoriana,
- **Zephriana,** Greek, West Wind, Reborn
- **Zoranna**, Zoriana,
- **Zacharee**, Zacharee,
- **Zaimir,** Zameer, Zameir, Hebrew, Song, Joyful
- **Zacary**, Zacc, Zaccari,
- **Zadok,** Zaydok, Hebrew, Righteous, Rewarded
- **Zoee**, Zoey, Zoia, Zoie,
- **Zackery**, Zackory,

- **Zimra**, Zamora, Zemora, Hebrew, Song of Praise, Thankful
- **Zandra,** Zahndra,
- **Zachary**, Zachrey,

# BONUS Chapter – Reader's Voted Favourites: Top 20 Girl Names

1. **Sophia,** Greek, Wisdom
2. **Emma,** Latin, Universal
3. **Olivia,** Latin, Olive tree
4. **Ava,** Hebrew, Life
5. **Mia,** Latin, Mine; bitter
6. **Isabella,** Hebrew, Pledged to God
7. **Aria,** Latin, Air, Lioness
8. **Zoe**, Greek, Life
9. **Charlotte,** Norse, Free man
10. **Lily**, English, English flower name
11. **Layla**, Arabic, Night
12. **Amelia,** Hebrew, Work
13. **Emily,** Latin, Rival
14. **Madelyn,** Hebrew, High tower or women from Magdala
15. **Adalynn**, English, Noble guardian
16. **Madison,** English, Son of Maud
17. **Chloe,** Greek, Young green shoot
18. **Harper**, English, Harp player
19. **Kaylee**, Celtic, Laurel, Crown

20. **Scarlett,** English, Red

# BONUS Chapter - Reader's Voted Favourites: Top 20 Boy Names

1. **Jackson**, English, Son of Jack
2. **Aiden**, Celtic, Fiery and little
3. **Oliver,** German, Olive tree
4. **Lucas**, Latin, Man from Luciana
5. **Liam**, German, Resolute protection
6. **Noah**, Hebrew, Comfort, Rest
7. **Ethan**, Hebrew, Firm, strong
8. **Mason,** French, Stoneworker
9. **Elijah,** Hebrew, Yahweh is God
10. **Grayson**, English, The son of the baliff
11. **Jacob,** Hebrew, Supplanter
12. **Michael,** Hebrew, Who is like God?
13. **Benjamin,** Hebrew, son of the right hand
14. **Carter,** English, Driver or cart maker
15. **James,** Hebrew, Supplanter
16. **Jayden,** Hebrew, God has heard
17. **Logan**, Celtic, Little hollow
18. **Alexander**, Greek, Defending men
19. **Caleb**, Hebrew, Devotion to God

20. **Ryan,** Celtic, Little king

# Conclusion

You here, you've made it to the end of the book. We sincerely hope that you've benefitted from this book. Perhaps you've found your perfect name, or you haven't quite decided yet. Hopefully, you at least have some prospects that you can think about. Our recommendation is to write them down on the following pages and to think about them for a couple of weeks. Say or shout the names outload and you will begin to get a feel for the names. Thank you very much for reading this book, we wish you all the best!

Can you do us a favor? If you have received any value from this book, would you be so kind to leave an honest review on Amazon? It would be very much appreciated.

*Write the names that you like here:*

_____

_____

_____

_____

_____

_____

_____

_____

_____

_____

_____

_____

Made in the USA
Lexington, KY
24 May 2017